T0305636

Social Entrepreneurship

Social Entrepreneurship: A Practical Introduction equips aspiring entrepreneurs with the tools needed to design and launch businesses to create positive social change in their communities. This accessible textbook aims to educate and motivate people interested in social entrepreneurship, showing that such businesses are a valuable part of the community development toolbox. Each chapter focuses on a key aspect of social entrepreneurship, from value creation and business planning to impact measurement and scaling up. Different social business models are presented, with analysis of their strengths and weaknesses. Cases and examples are included throughout the book and showcase real-life social enterprises in North America, South America, Europe, Australia, Africa, and the Caribbean. Discussion questions also support reflection and learning. A downloadable workbook offers support with checklists, social impact measurement, and other areas. An instructor manual containing test questions and experiential exercises is also available as a digital supplement for adopters. This book is ideal for introductory courses in social entrepreneurship and community development. It will also be valuable for those involved in social enterprises on the ground.

Rasheda L. Weaver, PhD is the Founder of Weaver's Social Enterprise Directory, a global social entrepreneurship training company based in the USA. She has worked as an Assistant Professor at the Hynes Institute for Entrepreneurship and Innovation at Iona College, USA and as an Assistant Professor of Community Entrepreneurship at the University of Vermont. Her expertise lies in the use of social enterprise and entrepreneurship as a tool for community economic development.

Social Entrepreneurship

A Practical Introduction

Rasheda L. Weaver

Routledge
Taylor & Francis Group

LONDON AND NEW YORK

Designed cover image: Getty

First published 2023
by Routledge
4 Park Square, Milton Park, Abingdon, Oxon OX14 4RN

and by Routledge
605 Third Avenue, New York, NY 10158

Routledge is an imprint of the Taylor & Francis Group, an informa business

© 2023 Rasheda L. Weaver

The right of Rasheda L. Weaver to be identified as author of this work has been asserted in accordance with sections 77 and 78 of the Copyright, Designs and Patents Act 1988.

All rights reserved. No part of this book may be reprinted or reproduced or utilised in any form or by any electronic, mechanical, or other means, now known or hereafter invented, including photocopying and recording, or in any information storage or retrieval system, without permission in writing from the publishers.

Trademark notice: Product or corporate names may be trademarks or registered trademarks, and are used only for identification and explanation without intent to infringe.

British Library Cataloguing-in-Publication Data
A catalogue record for this book is available from the British Library

ISBN: 9781032129464 (hbk)
ISBN: 9781032129433 (pbk)
ISBN: 9781003226963 (ebk)

DOI: 10.4324/9781003226963

Typeset in Bembo
by codeMantra

Access the Support Material: www.routledge.com/9781032129433

Contents

Acknowledgments

I thank Iona College and its Hynes Institute for Entrepreneurship and Innovation, the University of Vermont, Rutgers University-Camden, the Association for Research on Nonprofit Organizations and Voluntary Action (ARNOVA), the EMES International Research Network (EMES), and the United States Association for Small Business and Entrepreneurship (USASBE) for supporting my work. All of these organizations have advanced my development and confidence as a scholar by giving me platforms to utilize my gift and love for writing, research, teaching, and the overall advancement of human and community development.

I specifically would like to thank my colleagues at Iona College for the great contributions they have made to my life and work. Dr. Natalie Redcross, Dr. Michelle Veyvoda, Dr. Nadine Cosby, Dr. Yaliu He, Dr. Jennifer Kaalund, the entire Faculty of Color Circle at Iona College, and Danny Potocki. I thank you for your support, words of encouragement, and for being there when I needed it.

I thank my research assistants Chyanne Blakey, Riana Khan, and Maimouna Mbacke for the work we have done together throughout my years at Iona College and for their specific contributions to the development of this book. It has been a pleasure working with you and watching you evolve.

I thank my parents Angelina and Robert, my cousin Kenisha, my friends Daysi, Rene, Willa, and Chukwuma for being an amazing support system for me for years, but especially during the period through which this book was written. I went through great life challenges while producing this work. I thank you all for the advice and support that you gave me to help me overcome these challenges and to thrive in the midst of them.

I thank my children Benjamin Franklin and Havana Rose Weaver for being everything that they are. Not a day goes by that I don't feel joy from being their mother. Their beauty, warm spirits, big personalities, and short, but wise words beyond their age keep me humble, loyal, focused, and resilient. I love you.

I thank my late husband Alexander Weaver for being my champion and greatest supporter. I thank Alexander for believing in me and investing in me more than anyone in this world and for being my best friend.

Lastly, I would like to thank myself for not giving up on my dreams, regardless of any challenge that I encounter. I specifically thank my younger self for having a relentless self-confidence, courage, intellect, and love for humanity that fuels everything I do today. The most powerful weapon on Earth really is "the human soul on fire."

The Purpose of This Book

This book aims to answer a burning question that I have had for years...

If I teach good people how to make money, lots and lots of money, will they in return do tremendous good with it? Will they create deep and lasting impact in their own lives and in the lives of others? Will they inspire a new way of thinking about business, money, and positive social change?

I am striving to teach good people how to make money so I can see whether and how much good they do with it.

This book is just the beginning of a series of training programs, conferences, and global networking opportunities that seek to bolster the social entrepreneurship community worldwide.

Dr. Rasheda L. Weaver, PhD

Join me on this journey...
to connect commercial business strategies
to the heart and soul of social entrepreneurs.
Let's equip them to develop and launch sustainable social ventures.

Introduction

It is an interesting time to be alive. We are two decades past the millennium and societal problems are at an all-time high. This statement is evidenced by the fact that I started writing this book before the COVID-19 pandemic, which has been going on for two years and has no end in sight. While our world was faced with societal problems before, over 3 million people have now died due to the coronavirus worldwide, which is a highly transmissible respiratory virus that took the world by both surprise and storm in 2020.

Over the last two years, we have also endured a pandemic-induced economic recession due to most institutions having to close their doors to "stop the spread" of the coronavirus. As such, businesses are closing in record numbers, people are losing their homes or being evicted, and hunger is on the rise. Mental illness and domestic violence have also been increasing. In addition, historically marginalized racial and ethnic groups have been disproportionately affected by this virus and its effects on their communities. The world is also seeing dramatic climate changes that have resulted in certain regions being so hot that sea creatures in the ocean have died, tornadoes and hurricanes are devastating cities they once hardly occurred in, and snow is falling where it usually doesn't. All in all, the world is in a hard and strange place.

I once heard someone say that "if you're not angry, you're not paying attention." As a social scientist and professor who has studied and taught social enterprise and entrepreneurship for the last decade, I know that social enterprises are one strategy for combating these wicked social problems. Thus, I have written *Social Entrepreneurship: A Practical Introduction* in order to inspire, educate, and equip generations of positive social change agents with the tools they need to create economically sustainable social enterprises. I firmly believe that human beings are powerful and I have studied social entrepreneurs as they tackle all kinds of issues in their communities with courage and determination. My goal, in writing this book, is to facilitate and advance their work.

This textbook is a different kind of textbook. It is meant for use in both academic settings and by social entrepreneurs. It is thus written in a general format that fuses my personal life story, findings from my own research on social enterprises, and the latest research on social enterprise and social entrepreneurship around the world. The inspiration behind this book stems

DOI: 10.4324/9781003226963-1

from my childhood in the Bronx, New York. My parents are Jamaican and Cuban immigrants who came to the United States with nothing but a backpack and a dream – to birth and raise their children in the land of the opportunity. However, the neighborhood I grew up in was impoverished and crime-ridden. Growing up there inspired me to "be the change I wish to see in the world." I dreamed of starting a social enterprise (before I even knew of the term) that hired and paid new immigrants (like my parents) to work in a center I would establish called Dream Haven Community Research Center. Dream Haven would study the causes of poverty in my neighborhood and develop solutions to address them.

I was so passionate about this dream that I went to college, graduate school, and ultimately went on to pursue my doctorate to gain training as both a researcher (my life's passion) and a social entrepreneur to make Dream Haven a reality. However, I had a difficult time finding information on how to design, fund, and launch a social enterprise. There were no specific classes on the topic at the universities I attended, and the majority of research focused on case studies of particular social enterprises, but did not give me the depth of knowledge I needed to fulfill my dream. Thus, in 2017, I launched the first national study on the social, economic, and legal activities of social enterprises across the United States. My findings from researching 115 self-identifying social enterprises are the foundation of this book. However, I also pull information from the growing body of knowledge on this topic to present to you, my readers, a focused, thoughtful, and action-oriented handbook with insights from social enterprises around the world.

I was further inspired to create this book after the Mayor's Office of Grand Rapids, Michigan, invited me to serve as the keynote speaker for their annual Grand Rapids Neighborhood Summit, an event that educates and trains over 400 entrepreneurs and non-profit leaders in the city. After presenting my research, the audience desired more, practical knowledge (from me) about designing, operating, and understanding the impact of social enterprises on their communities. However, at that time, none of my work was provided in a format that the general public could easily consume or even access. It was only offered in academic journals that have a paywall. Furthermore, none of the books I have seen on the market provide the kind of evidenced-based information from my study in such a format as well. Thus, the goal of this book is to serve as a practical resource for aspiring and current social entrepreneurs in their mission to advance community economic development.

This book is organized into 12 chapters. Each chapter focuses on an important element in the complex world of social entrepreneurship, while providing case studies that illustrate these elements in the real world. In addition, discussion questions are provided for each chapter in order to challenge and spark the interest of readers. Tables and/or charts are also used in each chapter to ease understanding of the material and to attend to diverse reading styles.

Chapter 1 explains what the **terms** social enterprise, social entrepreneur, social entrepreneurship, and community entrepreneurship mean. It outlines why a growing number of policymakers, researchers, and practitioners believe that social entrepreneurship may be a tool for community development. Social enterprises are depicted in this chapter (and the book overall) as a social business intervention that combines social, economic, and sometimes environmental goals in order to foster positive social change in society. It delves into the social, legal, economic, and geographical characteristics of these businesses. In addition, the chapter explains how businesses of all sizes and industries are applying social entrepreneurship (and sometimes community entrepreneurship) and the impact it is having on the world.

Chapter 2 explores the **emergence of social enterprises all over the world**, but they emerge in different contexts for different reasons. Factors such as geographic context, social norms, socioeconomic status, and political context influence the design of social enterprise business models and their impact on beneficiaries. This chapter paints a picture of the diverse ecosystems for social enterprises globally. Readers will gain an understanding of how and why some contexts are abundant with social enterprises and support services, while others (that often seem in need of social enterprises) have few.

Chapter 3 outlines the importance of **researching consumer and beneficiary needs** before aiming to solve them through entrepreneurship. Research methods like community needs assessments, and contemporary entrepreneurial tools like Design Thinking and empathy mapping are explained in order to direct readers toward tools that may capture information about customer needs and interests. This chapter combines information from literature on market research with literature from community development and public policy in order to attend to the social and economic aspirations of aspiring social entrepreneurs.

Chapter 4 explores the relationship between **social enterprises and community development**. It distinguishes between community as a shared place/space and community as a shared idea across space and time. Social enterprises may view their communities based on a particular geographic boundary they seek to improve. They may also see their community as people who share the same passion for a social issue that they strive to combat. Regardless of whether a social enterprise has a place-based or issue-based sense of community, they have a reciprocal relationship with that community. This reciprocal relationship enables them to give value and receive a diversity of resources from that community as well. This chapter explains this relationship and outlines various community capitals that social enterprises may identify and acquire to strengthen their ventures.

Chapter 5 explores ten **different social impact models**, which are the strategies that social enterprises employ to combat social problems. A multitude of case studies are used to illustrate each social impact model. Models include the: (1) donation model; (2) social hiring model; (3) capacity building/ training; (4) social service or resource provision; (5) social procurement; (6) selling socially conscious products and services; (7) social marketing; (8) systemic change; (9) social movements; and (10) social finance services or products. This chapter is very applied in the sense that readers may use the knowledge to directly design a social enterprise.

Chapter 6 explores various **startup funding opportunities** and strategies available for social enterprises. It also examines challenges that social enterprises may face acquiring certain types of financing and how to overcome them. Given the flexible legal structure of social enterprises, this chapter aims to guide readers through the financial landscape that is available to entrepreneurs and organizational leaders in general, regardless of the legal structure. Topics such as crowdfunding, social impact bonds, venture capitalists, angel investors, impact investors, alternative grassroots–style fundraising (e.g. Jamaican partner system), and more will be described.

Chapter 7 outlines various **revenue models and income streams** for social businesses. Case studies are used throughout the chapter to illustrate the variety of ways that entrepreneurship can advance social causes through innovative and traditional revenue models. Readers of this chapter will gain a deep overview of the myriad of ways that social enterprises and institutions in general can generate revenue needed to support their operations and growth.

Chapter 8 explains the difference between **business planning** for a commercial enterprise and a social enterprise. The chapter discusses and explains the common elements of a traditional business plan for both types of enterprises. In addition, new business planning tools like the lean business model canvas and the social business model canvas are provided. Furthermore, this chapter explains innovative social enterprise business planning organizations such as accelerators and incubators. Lastly, this chapter outlines a checklist of things to do once a business plan is complete and it's time to launch a social enterprise.

Chapter 9 emphasizes the importance of **social impact measurement**. It outlines various quantitative and qualitative tools for measuring the social outcomes of social enterprise work. However, special attention is paid to how the capability approach, a multidimensional framework for viewing poverty, may be used to re-conceptualize social value creation. This list presents Dr. Weaver's List of Central Social Capabilities that is used to organize and evaluate the kinds of social impact that social enterprises may create.

Chapter 10 discusses scaling a social enterprise in terms of growing the organization itself and in terms of growing its social impact. Three different models for **scaling a social enterprise** with an emphasis on cultivating human resources are discussed. The models relate to human capital acquisition, human capital development, and human capital retention. Human capital acquisition involves recruiting staff with essential skills and mindsets. Human capital development consists of training and rewarding employees. Human capital retention is the process of striving to keep employees for long periods of time, often through incentive packages and benefits. Other considerations for scaling social enterprises such as expanding social impact via surface-level and deep-level strategies are also discussed.

Chapter 11 prepares readers for the **common challenges** of running a social enterprise. It also discusses factors that may increase their chances of success. Challenges include access to finance and investment, recruiting and retaining talented staff, managing a social enterprise in the growth stages, and setting prices and managing cash flow. **Success factors** include developing a strong social network, being dedicated to the venture's success, securing seed capital, the acceptance of the venture idea in the public discourse, the ability of the service to stand the market test, and the entrepreneur's previous managerial experience. In addition to discussing the challenges and success factors, the chapter explains ways to overcome the challenges, as well as how to set the conditions needed for success.

Chapter 12 explores the different **legal structures** that social enterprises operate under. It emphasizes the importance of viewing legal structure as a strategy that helps social enterprises capture different kinds of resources and opportunities in their context. The strengths and weaknesses of operating a social enterprise as a for-profit business, non-profit organization, or under a hybrid law are also outlined.

Lastly, the conclusion outlines the central argument of this book, which is that social enterprises are a social intervention in the form of business that must be economically sustainable. With that said, this book aims to equip people with the desire to utilize social enterprises as tools for creating positive social change in their communities with the knowledge needed to accomplish their goals. Social entrepreneurs, in essence, are people who believe in civic engagement. Research shows that many social entrepreneurs have either experienced or witnessed someone experiencing the social problems they seek to combat. As such, they develop social enterprises as a way to "create the world they want to see." This book ends with a list of important notes for social entrepreneurs to remember throughout their entrepreneurial journey. By educating people with this knowledge, they will have the tools needed to embark on a career or lifestyle that enables them to positively influence the world.

1 What Is Social Entrepreneurship?

Social entrepreneurship is a hot topic. Around the world, a growing number of policymakers, researchers, and practitioners believe that social enterprise may be a tool for creating positive social change. While the field has been around for over 50 years, the last two decades has been transformational. Social enterprises have increased in number and exist in virtually all industries. In addition, organizations like Ashoka, The Social Enterprise World Forum, Social Enterprise UK, and Social Enterprise Scotland have been created to facilitate social enterprise startup and operation activities. Dozens, if not, hundreds of colleges and universities have created entire programs that train students to "change the world" by creating socially conscious businesses. Research in the field has skyrocketed. Policymakers and other entrepreneurial support organizations have created seed funding initiatives and investment opportunities to help launch social ventures. Non-academic training programs such as coworking spaces, accelerators, and social enterprise consulting firms are also on the rise. All in all, social entrepreneurship is a bustling field. However, there is much debate about what the concept itself really even means.

In this book, we define **social entrepreneurship** *as the process of using commercial business techniques to generate revenue that is used to combat social problems.* The term social enterprise refers to the *organizations* engaging in the process of combating social problems using entrepreneurial activity. These organizations can be for-profit businesses, nonprofit organizations, or a combination of both organizational structures. The creators of social enterprises are social entrepreneurs, most of whom have a prosocial attitude toward creating a better world. Many have also experienced or witnessed the effects of the social issues they strive to combat today and aim to be a part of creating positive changes in society.

What distinguishes social enterprises from traditional for-profit businesses or nonprofit organizations is their desire to engage in entrepreneurial activity while having an underlying social purpose that drives and guides their decision making and work. For my dissertation research, I studied the social, economic, and legal activities of 115 self-identifying social enterprises. While they differ in terms of the social problems they strive to address, their legal structure, and their location, the main thing they all have in common is that they utilize some or all of their revenue and profits to develop products, programs, or initiatives that seek to alleviate social problems.

DOI: 10.4324/9781003226963-2

Other characteristics that social enterprises share include: (1) having a dual or triple (environmental) bottom-line approach to business, (2) being locally embedded in communities, (3) addressing a diversity of social problems, and (4) having a flexible organizational structure. The following sections discuss these characteristics.

Dual or Triple Bottom-Line

Social enterprises have a "dual bottom-line" approach to business. In business, the term "bottom-line" signifies the total on the bottom of a financial report that shows a business' net profit or loss. The bottom-line determines whether or not business owners or shareholders will make a profit. A dual bottom-line structure, however, consists of a social and an economic mission. The social mission consists of creating public/social good. The economic mission involves creating "private gain" for the business. The social mission focuses on providing services, products, or developing organizations that address problems affecting people and society. It also involves identifying and alleviating the root causes of social problems, making the business publicly beneficial. The economic mission involves generating revenue in an effort to sustain the social enterprise. Through this dual bottom-line structure, social enterprises aim to generate revenue that, at least in part, finances their social programs and interests.

There are social enterprises that suggest they have a "triple bottom-line" approach to business, wherein the third bottom-line focuses on addressing environmental challenges. Some people refer to this triple bottom-line as a focus on "people, planet, and profit." Nevertheless, social enterprises, overall, strive to improve societal issues.

Given their socially conscious nature, it is no wonder that a great deal of people are interested in their work. In a TED Talk entitled "Why Business Can Be Good at Solving Social Problems" (viewed over 2.5 million times), Harvard Business School Professor Michael E. Porter argues that businesses may be the best institutional form for combating social problems. Though businesses traditionally focus on generating profits for their shareholders and have been a cause of various societal issues (e.g. inequality), Professor Porter argues that businesses are the only institutions that create wealth and value. This "economic value creation factor" makes social enterprises an attractive tool for creating social change. Why? Because unlike traditional nonprofit organizations that often rely on grants to fund their initiatives, social enterprises have the potential to sustain themselves. More than half of the social enterprises I have studied generate more than $500,000 annually, and approximately 30% generate over $1 million each year. This revenue has equipped them to help more than 1 million Americans, and those are just the ones in my study alone.

Geographically Embedded at the Local Level

Given their focus on alleviating social problems, most social enterprises operate at the local level. Naturally, it is easier to tackle societal challenges like unemployment, urban blight, and poverty at the local level than to create a nationwide initiative that substantially addresses issues at a deep level. In addition, social entrepreneurs have usually been personally affected by the issues they seek to combat or have witnessed other people experience them. Thus, the organizations they create are often responses to personal adversity, which happens locally.

Operating at a local level is often a strategic decision among social entrepreneurs because it facilitates the creation of reciprocal relationships with their communities. They work with local government to obtain resources, spread awareness about their businesses, or to implement an initiative. They may also hire and seek volunteers locally. Some social enterprises, like the Social Enterprise Greenhouse in Rhode Island and Social Enterprise UK in the United Kingdom, even work with legislators to develop laws that facilitate their work.

On the other hand, there are social enterprises that start small and grow to become large, renowned companies. Newman's Own is a popular example of a large social enterprise. It is a for-profit business that sells food products such as pasta sauce, mints, lemonade, and more. All of its profits are donated to various charities through its Newman's Own Foundation. Another example of a large social enterprise is the eco-friendly household and baby product company Seventh Generation. Created in 1988, Seventh Generation is viewed as one of the most environmentally conscious corporations in the United States. It was purchased by Unilever in 2017 for approximately $700 million. Thus, while many social enterprises have less than ten employees, there are some large companies that have had a social mission from their start or that have acquired one over time. I expect that as the field grows, we will see more small social enterprises scaling up in terms of their revenue generation, number of employees, and the reach of their social impact.

Addressing a Diversity of Social Problems

Social enterprises strive to address a diversity of social issues, including unemployment, environmental pollution, food waste, poverty, and more. While studies on their impact are limited, there is a growing body of evidence that shows that social enterprises are particularly useful for social hiring, which is the intentional hiring of people from vulnerable populations. These populations may include the formerly incarcerated, homeless people, undocumented residents, people living in poverty, and the under-educated and under-skilled.

Research has shown that social hiring can improve employee skills, economic self-sufficiency, professional development, and social capital. Others have found that it advances health maintenance and improves rates of stable housing for their employees. Lastly, employees at affirmative business social enterprises show a decrease in health and substance abuse issues, as well as a decrease in their dependence on government welfare programs.

While we know social hiring is an impactful social enterprise strategy, there is more work to be done in regard to assessing the many other strategies that social enterprises employ to address social issues. Of the 115 social enterprises in my study, the average social enterprise aims to combat about three different types of social problems. However, they usually do not develop these programs all at once. Instead, as their revenue increases, they develop more products, programs, or initiatives over time.

Flexible Organizational Structure

As aforementioned, social enterprises may be nonprofit organizations, for-profit businesses, or a combination of both known as hybrid organizations. The organizational and legal form that social enterprises operate under are strategic decisions. Having a hybrid model, for instance, can help social enterprises utilize the strengths of both legal forms. The for-profit business helps social enterprises generate revenue from unrestricted sources. The nonprofit organization may help social enterprises obtain grants and save money on property-related expenses, sales, and other taxes (Figure 1.1).

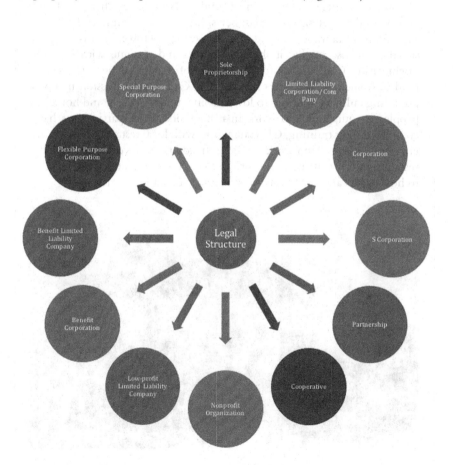

Figure 1.1 Legal Structure.

Combining both of these legal forms to create positive social change can lead to great results, as mentioned in the case of Newman's Own. However, legal challenges that stem from combining these two organizational structures have inspired the creation of various social enterprise laws. Social enterprise legal forms include the: Benefit Corporation (B-Corporation), Low-Profit Limited Liability Company (L3C), Social Purpose Corporation (SPC), and the Benefit Limited Liability Company (BLLC). These new legal forms are tailored to the use of business for social good. They are all for-profit businesses that enable their directors and shareholders to engage in publicly beneficial activities without consequence (more on this in Chapter 12).

Case in Point: CK Café

CK Cafe is a social enterprise in Camden, New Jersey that sells foods such as sandwiches, salads, and desserts. It generates commercial revenue through its restaurant sales and catering services. However, it is a hybrid social enterprise in that it shares resources and revenue with its sister organization Cathedral Kitchen, a nonprofit soup kitchen that serves food to homeless people in Camden. CK Cafe's social mission involves providing culinary training to low-income, under-skilled, and homeless people to equip them to work in restaurants. Once participants have completed their training, CK Cafe works with local restaurants in southern New Jersey to find work for them. In addition to working with local restaurants, CK Cafe partners with the local government and universities to host events and field visits for students and faculty (Figure 1.2).

Figure 1.2 CK Cafe.
Source: Catholic Herald Star.

Conclusion

A social enterprise is in essence a form of civic engagement. It involves citizens utilizing business as a tool for advancing positive social change. A social enterprise, itself, is an intervention that combines social, economic, and (sometimes) environmental goals to create changes in society. It is a part of a growing movement toward conscious capitalism, which recognizes the damage businesses have and can inflict on society. As a result, a growing number of business leaders are striving to make business practices more inclusive, socially conscious, and environmentally beneficial. An increasing number of consumers also aim to influence the role that businesses play in positive social change. They are watching and responding to the actions of businesses in the United States and throughout the world.

The diversity of the social problems that social enterprises combat, their legal structure, and the ways they generate revenue make their potential for addressing societal problems appealing to many audiences. Their embeddedness at the local level is also inspirational. In the famous words of Mahatma Gandhi, it makes people feel like they can "be the change they want to see in the world." However, as you will see in Chapter 2, who and what social enterprises were at the time of their emergence in the United States back in the 1970s is quite different from the force they are today.

Resources

The resources provided below are of major social enterprise educational and support organizations in the United States. Explore their work to learn more about social enterprises.

Weaver's Social Enterprise Directory (http://socialenterprisedirectory.com/)
Weaver's Social Enterprise Directory is a national, online directory that features information about the geographic location, social activities, goods and services, and legal characteristics of social enterprises throughout the United States. The directory features information on over 1,000 social enterprises in the nation.

Ashoka (https://www.ashoka.org/en-us/focus/social-entrepreneurship)
Since 1980, Ashoka has been a leading organization in the development of social entrepreneurship as a field. It is a community of social entrepreneurs and proponents of the field that provide educational opportunities and competitions related to supporting social entrepreneurs.

The Aspen Institute (https://www.aspeninstitute.org/about/)
The Aspen Institute is an organization that focuses on advancing knowledge related to education and policy. Its website provides case studies, resources, training program information, and research articles on social entrepreneurship and the role of business in society.

Social Enterprise Alliance (https://socialenterprise.us/)
The Social Enterprise Alliance is a leading membership organization for work on social enterprise in the United States. It has various member chapters across the nation and provides workshops, webinars, and networking events on social enterprise.

B Lab (https://bcorporation.net/)
B Lab is a nonprofit organization that awards B Corp certification to for-profit businesses that have a social mission. While based in Pennsylvania, its members are businesses all over the world. B Lab has been a driving force behind the development and advancement of the Benefit Corporation legal business entity in the United States.

2 The Emergence of Social Enterprise across the World

Chapter 1 discusses how many social entrepreneurs have seen or witnessed the social problems they face up close and personally. However, many people have also experienced social problems and just live with the experience. Researchers have thus sought to discover why some people seek to transform their social problems into opportunities for positive social change, while many just endure them. They examine contextual, cultural, and socioeconomic factors that influence social entrepreneurship activity around the world. We've learned that social enterprise business models differ by geographic region and are influenced by the culture and resources within each region. For example, the United States is an individualistic, innovation-driven economy so social enterprises in the United States emphasize revenue generation. The United States does not have free, universal healthcare or education. In regard to poverty, there is a strong gap between the wealthy and the poor. These are all reasons that thrust Americans into entrepreneurship and influence the business model they choose. In Europe, however, there is a relatively strong social safety net that manifests in substantial assistance for issues like unemployment, launching new businesses, free healthcare, and free education. These supports make it easier for many people to *not* engage in entrepreneurship and for people that choose an entrepreneurial path to take advantage of revenue sources like government subsidies, grants, and contracts.

In other words, the reason people engage in entrepreneurship of any kind differs based on the level and management of individual and community-level social problems in their geographic area. Social enterprises exist all over the world, but they emerge in different contexts for different reasons. This chapter takes you on an exploration of the major components of social enterprise ecosystems and how they help or hinder the development of social entrepreneurship in a region. You will gain an understanding of how and why some contexts are abundant with social enterprises and support services, while others (that often seem in need of social enterprises) have little.

Social Enterprise Emergence and Context

The commonality among all social enterprises is that they strive to combat social issues. However, the business and social impact models they tend to

DOI: 10.4324/9781003226963-3

implement to achieve this goal differ by context. Context consists of the history, politics, laws, media, cultural, economic, and social influences within a community, area, or region. Contextual factors deeply influence social enterprises and their role as drivers of community development. Context influences the resources available, the mindset that drives more or less people to engage in entrepreneurship, and the ways that entrepreneurs design their business models. It also influences the appropriate techniques for addressing social issues (e.g. receptivity). For example, social enterprises, while revenue-generating organizations, may be expected to redistribute a certain number of profits back into the organization (as opposed to directing it to owners or shareholders) in certain contexts. Whereas, in other contexts, social enterprises are not expected to do so.

Research has shown that context has a profound influence on the emergence and propensity of social enterprises. There are two major theories that seek to explain how and why social enterprises emerge. The first is institutional voids (IVs) theory, which suggests that social enterprises tend to develop in communities where there are absent and/or weak institutions that prevent poor people from addressing their basic human needs. These voids are opportunity spaces for social entrepreneurs. Social entrepreneurs in IV contexts aim to increase self-sufficiency of the impoverished. Social entrepreneurs use bricolage (making do with what is at hand) to achieve their goals in contexts where institutional voids exist. As such, entrepreneurs and organizations collaborate to meet diverse social needs in a cost-effective manner.

The second theory suggests that social enterprises develop in contexts where there is high institutional support in general. Specifically, contexts where there is high government activity in regard to alleviating social problems. These theorists suggest that social enterprises are not driven by the *propensity* of social issues in a given area. Instead, they are driven by the *existence* of social issues coupled with government support that help social enterprises address them. Government is viewed by institutional support theorists as a partner to social enterprise.

In my own research on social enterprises, my findings have led me to introduce *institutional sufficiency theory* as an alternative explanation for the institutional contexts where social enterprises emerge. Institutional sufficiency theory suggests that social enterprises develop in contexts that have substantial human need, as well as the opportunity to acquire resources that social enterprises may utilize to combat them. Social enterprises need a foundation to develop and grow, but they also require a human need to address. I believe that distressed communities, those that lack resources, are unlikely to attract and retain social entrepreneurs despite their dire needs. If they do, they will most likely operate as or with a nonprofit organization that may attract external resources from donors because the local economy limits revenue-generation opportunities. Similarly, affluent communities have resources, but little needs for social entrepreneurs to address. In essence, institutional sufficiency theory argues that the hybrid structure of social enterprise calls

Table 2.1 Comparison of Current Institutional Theories

	Institutional Voids	*Institutional Support*	*Institutional Sufficiency*
Theory	Social enterprises develop where social needs are abundant	Social enterprises develop where government support is high	Social enterprises develop in context where they can meet their dual goals
Method of investigation	Case studies	Large sample	Medium sample
Research context (where the study took place)	Developing countries	Global	United States
Unit of measurement/ analysis	Individual social enterprises	Social entrepreneurs/ social enterprises	Various social enterprises

for a hybrid context for its operation. Social entrepreneurs need serious issues to address *and* the resources necessary to address them (Table 2.1).

Social Enterprise Activity and Ecosystems

The Global Entrepreneurship Monitor's research on social enterprise activity in 49 countries found that social enterprise activity is higher in contexts where entrepreneurial activity is also high. Social enterprise activity is also increasing at a faster *rate* than commercial enterprise activity. As a field, social entrepreneurship has been around for over 50 years, but it has skyrocketed in growth over the last 20 years. As such, many scholars and business leaders argue that it is the *future* of business. Yet, this statement is controversial because while all social enterprises engage in commercial, revenue-generating activity, they are not all businesses. Some social enterprises are nonprofit organizations. Nevertheless, Figure 2.1 shows that the United States has the highest rates of social enterprise and the Caribbean, Latin America, and Africa have higher rates than most other areas as well. Interestingly, however, areas like the United Kingdom, Australia, and Canada have some of the most robust and supportive social enterprise ecosystems in the world.

Social entrepreneurs are influenced, stimulated, and at times even hindered by a broader entrepreneurial ecosystem. An **entrepreneurial ecosystem** is a community of interdependent actors, institutions, and systems that work together to create and grow businesses. Entrepreneurship ecosystems have distinct social and geographic characteristics. They are complex, include a diversity of players, and they stimulate entrepreneurial activity. They work well when members of the ecosystem interact in a way that creates a foundation

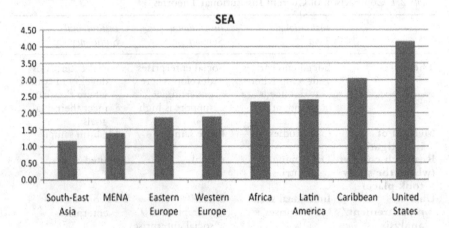

Figure 2.1 Prevalence of Early Stage Social Entrepreneurship Activity (SEA) by Region.

Source: Lepoutre, J., Justo, R., Terjesen, S., & Bosma, N. (2013). Designing a global standardized methodology for measuring social entrepreneurship activity: The Global Entrepreneurship Monitor social entrepreneurship study. *Small Business Economics, 40*(3), 693–714.

for the development and growth of businesses. Both the individual entrepreneur and the ecosystem are important. Given that social entrepreneurship is one type of entrepreneurship, it is often situated in the midst of a broader entrepreneurial ecosystem. However, around the world, an increasing number of leaders in the field are laser focused on creating a foundation for strong social entrepreneurship ecosystems.

A **social enterprise ecosystem** can be defined as an interconnected network or community of people and educational, political, social, and financial institutions dedicated to fostering social entrepreneurship. They may include support systems such as social enterprise certification marks, labels, and registrations, legal structures, business development and support services, funding networks, impact measurement and reporting systems, and social finance and investment opportunities. These ecosystems are abundant in some regions, but barely exist in other regions. While this distinction is important to note, as an optimist and true believer in the power of social entrepreneurship, I see an abundance of potential opportunities for motivated people in this field.

Figure 2.2 is an example of the relationship between context, social enterprises, and the different kinds of capital within a social enterprise ecosystem. Chapter 4 describes **community capitals** in detail, but they may be defined as the financial and non-financial resources that exist in communities and contribute to community development. Community capitals are used to leverage financial and non-financial resources that aid in social enterprise establishment and growth.

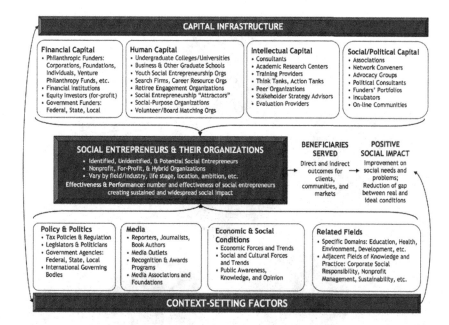

Figure 2.2 Social Enterprise Ecosystem Map Example.
Source: Center for the Advancement of Social Entrepreneurship at Duke University.
Note: This figure is not all-inclusive.

Important Ecosystem Features

The World Economic Forum outlines eight pillars of successful entrepreneurial ecosystems, including accessible markets, workforce, funding, mentors, government, education, cultural support, and universities as catalysts. These pillars are embedded in the descriptions of important ecosystem features below.

Business Training and Technical Support Services. In recent years, a variety of business training programs and technical support services targeting social entrepreneurs have emerged around the world. The four main types of programs and services are accelerator programs, business incubators, fellowship programs, and college and university programs. Each is owned and operated by different parties with distinct goals on how they train aspiring social entrepreneurs (Figure 2.3).

Accelerator Programs. The book *Observing Acceleration: Uncovering the Effects of Accelerators on Impact-Oriented Entrepreneurs* by Saurabh Lall, PhD, and Peter Roberts, PhD, explores the increasing growth of impact-oriented accelerator programs. Accelerator programs are fixed-term, cohort-based business education and planning programs that often include seed investment, networking opportunities, mentorship, and opportunities to pitch business ideas to possible funders. For example, GrowthAfrica is an accelerator in

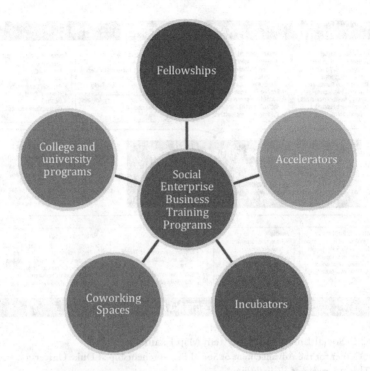

Figure 2.3 Types of Social Enterprise Business Training Programs.

Nairobi, Kenya, that works with social entrepreneurs in Kenya, Uganda, and Ethiopia. It has been operating for over two decades to assist entrepreneurs with business development, coaching, financial modeling, investment readiness, and more. It has worked with over 240 ventures and has raised over $60 million in investment revenue and grants for the startups they work with. Accelerator programs like GrowthAfrica provide a motivational community and resources that aim to facilitate the launch of social ventures.

Incubators. Incubators are similar to accelerator programs in that they provide entrepreneurship training and education; however, the time duration is usually longer. They also may or may not have a cohort model. For example, the Halcyon Incubator in Washington, DC, in the United States offers the Halcyon Flagship Residential Fellowship that provides five months of free housing, a stipend for personal spending, and a coworking space. However, many incubators just provide a workspace or office for social entrepreneurs to run their companies in addition to offering technical and other business support services.

Fellowships. While social entrepreneurship has been around for over 50 years, the average person on Earth is not familiar with the term. It is not yet a "household" concept. Yet, the potential for social entrepreneurship as a tool for advancing positive social change is great in a world where societal issues seem to keep piling up. As such, numerous fellowship programs exist to help social entrepreneurs develop and grow their organizations. Fellowships usually have a cohort model where like-minded social entrepreneurs may incubate and grow their ideas together over a given amount of time. Many fellowships also offer financial stipends and some even offer housing. These types of incentives help remove barriers to the kinds of people who may participate in such programs, as financial and residential challenges may preclude aspiring entrepreneurs from having the time to participate. Some examples of popular social enterprise fellowships include: Echoing Green Fellowship, Aspen Global Leadership Network Fellowships, and The Ashoka Fellowship.

College and University Programs. A growing number of universities and colleges have developed courses, degree programs, and social enterprise pitching competitions to educate and elevate future generations of social entrepreneurs. Some, like Sheffield Hallam University in Sheffield, England, even have pop-up shop locations where students can run their entrepreneurial venture. Universities and colleges are regarded as major catalysts for social entrepreneurship, as many people are introduced to the term first in a college setting (most social entrepreneurs have at least a college-level education). In addition, universities and colleges are a mecca for education and innovation. They are often great partners for social entrepreneurs looking to share or discover resources (e.g. students for internships, researchers to evaluate a program) needed to bring their entrepreneurial ideas to life. Furthermore, universities and colleges train the workforce through which entrepreneurs will acquire their employees and other human resources and partners.

Certification marks, labels, and registrations. In recent years, more and more organizations have been adopting certifications and labels that publicly identify them as respected organizations that meet specific standards associated with a given label. Government and organization certifications like the USDA label and Fair Trade label distinguish products with the label from others as meeting specific requirements for food and body products outlined by the United States Department of Agriculture and the Fair World Project (Figures 2.4 and 2.5).

In the world of social enterprise, a number of labels and certifications have been developed to distinguish social enterprises as meeting a particular definition, impact measurement qualifications, and/or profit distribution requirements. Table 2.2 shows several social enterprise labels used in different parts of the world. Like the field, these marks and certifications are new and evolving. As such, they may change over time.

Legal structures around the world. Social enterprises may legally operate as nonprofit organizations, for-profit businesses, or a combination of both organizational forms. They may be established under traditional for-profit structures like a sole proprietorship or limited liability company and as a nonprofit organization. Over the last 15 years, new types of legal forms have also been developed to support the social and economic goals of social enterprises such as the: Community Interest Company (CIC), Benefit Corporation, the

Figure 2.4 USDA Label.

Figure 2.5 Fair Trade Label.

Table 2.2 Examples of Social Enterprise Labels

Issuer	Buy Social Canada Label	Buy Social UK	B Lab	Social Traders Certification
Label				
Source	buysocialcanada.com	socialenterprise.org.uk	Bcorporation.net	Socialtraders.com.au

Low-Profit Limited Liability Company (L3C), the Benefit Limited Liability Company (Benefit LLC), and the Social Purpose Corporation (SPC). These new legal forms, often referred to as hybrid laws, enable social enterprises to operate as for-profit businesses (minus the CIC) that *prioritize* their social mission over profit. They differ by the number of profits distributed to shareholders, their transparency and public reporting requirements, and the level at which they prioritize their social goals. Ultimately, all social enterprises (regardless of legal form) balance a dual bottom-line structure consisting of their social and economic goals. Social enterprise legal structures are discussed in depth in Chapter 12.

Government Policies. Several national and regional government entities have developed polices that support the identification, establishment, growth, and funding of social enterprises in their geographic area. Some government bodies allocate funding for social enterprises, develop hybrid legal forms, establish national social enterprise registries, and require social enterprise impact measurement. Each nation is at a different stage in its history with social entrepreneurship. Not to mention, different social, cultural, governmental, and economic characteristics within a region may influence the frequency of social enterprises in that region and how they take shape and form.

Membership and Support Networks. Membership and support networks for social enterprises are an important medium for the development of a social enterprise community, especially within a particular geographic area. They tend to develop in areas where there is substantial social enterprise activity, which then inspires the need to organize a community around such activity. Membership and support networks may offer supports such as social entrepreneur meetups, online or in-person shopping markets to sell social enterprise goods, annual conferences, regional meetups, workshops, advocacy and policy work, funding opportunities with investors, and more. Some examples of social enterprise membership and support organizations include: The Social Enterprise Alliance (United States of America), SE Ontario (Ontario Region of Canada), Social Enterprise Scotland (Scotland), Social Enterprise UK (United Kingdom), and the Queensland Social Enterprise Council (Australia).

Impact measurement and reporting systems. Measuring and reporting social impact is important for understanding the effectiveness of the social and/or environmental activities that are at the heart of social enterprise work. However, depending on the kind of organization, measuring social impact can be difficult and thus many social entrepreneurs forgo measuring impact altogether. For example, in my study of 115 social entrepreneurs in the United States, less than 50% measured their social impact. However, various types of impact measurement tools exist, and they come in both qualitative and quantitative form. Measuring social impact can be important for acquiring government contracts and grants, obtaining foundation grants, and fulfilling the expectations of socially minded consumers, including individuals, families, businesses, and nonprofit organizations. As awareness about social entrepreneurship grows, people naturally desire to understand the where and how social enterprises are reducing social problems (more on this in Chapter 9).

Social finance and investment opportunities. Social enterprise is an emerging field that has inspired innovations in how, what, and why organizations are financed. While financing for social projects such as grants and donations is not a new idea or initiative, the field of social entrepreneurship has inspired a variety of new opportunities for financing the alleviation of social ills. The term social finance is a form of sustainable finance that refers to funding opportunities that are designed to address social and environmental problems, often with a financial return for its investors. University of Oxford Professor of Social Entrepreneurship Alex Nicholls compiled the list in Table 2.3 of types of sustainable finance and related terms. As shown in the table, there are various types of innovative funding opportunities related to social and environmental outcomes. Such opportunities are essential to the growth of the social enterprise ecosystem as they provide funding for social entrepreneurs throughout different stages of their entrepreneurial journey.

Table 2.3 Types of Sustainable Finance

Type of Finance	Example Organization
Grants	Rockefeller Foundation
Venture philanthropy	New Philanthropy
Program-related investment	Ford Foundation
Mission-related investment	KL Felicitas Foundation
Development finance	Centers for Disease Control and Prevention
Ethical finance	Faith Invest
Social (impact) finance	RBC Wealth Management
Green finance	Resonance Fund
Impact finance	Bridges Fund Management
Socially responsible finance	Nutmeg

Source: Nicholls, A. Sustainable Finance: A Primer and Recent Developments.

Conclusion

While an entrepreneurial ecosystem engages diverse stakeholders, institutions, and individuals in the creation and growth of businesses, it is the individual entrepreneurs who must venture to launch new organizations. Entrepreneurial intention and action are inspired by the prevalence of needs that demand fulfilling, along with the availability of resources and support systems that facilitate entrepreneurial pursuit.

Social entrepreneurship is a growing phenomenon around the world. As such, as a reader of this book, you are among a new generation of people who are learning about this evolving field of entrepreneurship. Before exploring the components of social enterprise ecosystems, it is important to note that they look different depending on their context. In Europe, for instance, social enterprise pioneers have helped develop various social enterprise laws (e.g. Belgium, Italy), fiscal incentive and investment opportunities, business development coaching and support services, and opportunities for social procurement dedicated to serving social enterprises. In the United States, four types of "hybrid laws" have been enacted since 2008.

Some regions have more supports for social enterprise development, and some have less. Ultimately, the voids that exist in a region's social enterprise ecosystem present the opportunity for them to be filled.

3   Assessing Needs to Create Value

When entrepreneurs create value for their consumers through the services and products they sell, they simultaneously create value for themselves. According to the Merriam-Webster dictionary, value is defined as "the relative worth, utility, or importance" of something. Value is essential to entrepreneurship. When entrepreneurs *continuously* identify, understand, and meet consumer needs, consumers continuously need and value them in return. In my entrepreneurship classes, I tell my students "don't aim for one and done revenue. Aim for recurring revenue." However, recurring revenue may only be achieved when an entrepreneur prioritizes continuous learning about their consumers' needs and the creation of solutions that actually meet them.

The term value proposition refers to the value delivered to a consumer when they buy or receive a product or service. This chapter describes the importance of researching human needs before aiming to solve them through entrepreneurship. It explores entrepreneurial tools like Design Thinking and empathy mapping in order to direct readers toward tools that capture information about customer needs and interests. It also examines different research methods like community needs assessments and the social capability intervention model that deepen understanding of social needs and strategies for meeting them. This chapter combines research from business and entrepreneurship with research from community development and public policy in order to attend to the social and economic aspirations of social entrepreneurs.

As organizations with dual goals, social enterprises must ensure they are selling products and services that are valuable enough for consumers to purchase. In addition, they also have the responsibility of creating social programs or products that enhance the life of their beneficiaries. The dual goals needed to successfully operate a social enterprise forces a deep understanding of the needs of the various consumers they serve, which may be more challenging. However, it also enables them to create dual impact.

Types of Consumers

One of the first steps to identifying, understanding, and meeting consumer needs is the recognition that there are different types of consumers (e.g.

DOI: 10.4324/9781003226963-4

customers, users, beneficiaries). The customer is the person who pays for a product or service. They have the purchasing power and thus certain needs (e.g. product price) of theirs must be satisfied. However, the end user is the person who will *use* a product or service. For example, parents buy their children toys, but the children are the end users while the parents are the customers. Both consumer types must be satisfied, but in different ways. Children desire toys that bring them joy and entertainment, while the parents purchasing them need the toys to be affordable in addition to entertaining.

In social entrepreneurship, however, there is a third consumer type to consider – the beneficiary. A beneficiary is a person who benefits or gains from something. Beneficiaries differ from both customers and end users in that they may never even interact with an organization's products or services at all, yet they may benefit from it in various ways. Sometimes, the customer, end user, and beneficiary are all the same. However, they often are not (Figure 3.1).

Frank Water CIC, for example, is a social enterprise in the United Kingdom that sells products like water bottles, bottled water, and gifts to the general public in the United Kingdom, but also to people who purchase from their website. While their customers mainly come from the United Kingdom, their beneficiaries are the communities in India and Nepal that benefit from them providing safe drinking water, which is scarce in these communities. Beneficiaries may benefit from a social enterprise in various ways, including socially, culturally, financially, politically, legally, mentally, and spiritually. It really just depends on the social services provided by a social enterprise and the outcomes of those services on beneficiary lives.

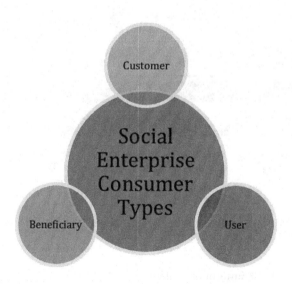

Figure 3.1 Consumer Types.

Human-Centered Design for Market Research

In recent years, the field of entrepreneurship has had a growing interest and value in human-centered design. Human-centered design prioritizes the understanding of human needs as a pre-requisite to developing the entrepreneurial solutions that meet them. Human-centered design debunks the idea that entrepreneurs have some grand idea that immediately meets consumer needs and becomes the next business empire. Instead, the approach recognizes that entrepreneurship takes time and creativity. Time is needed to understand consumers and creativity is needed to innovatively address their needs through entrepreneurial solutions.

The process of human-centered design is comprised of the following three major phases: (1) inspiration, (2) ideation, and (3) implementation. Inspiration involves doing research on consumer needs and trying to understand their problems and desires. It also involves understanding their experiences purchasing products or services that are an entrepreneur's or that are similar. In the inspiration phase, entrepreneurs focus on understanding their user's experience and the emotional realties that inform or influence their purchasing decisions.

Once entrepreneurs empathize with their consumers and have a firm theory of what their needs, challenges, and desires are, they may then move to the ideation phase. The ideation phase involves creatively generating as many ideas as possible. In this phase, it is important to not judge, evaluate, or discard of any ideas too quickly (see Figure 3.2 for brainstorming rules). Instead, brainstorming as many ideas as possible is essential. Once an entrepreneur has generated many ideas about how to solve their consumer's need, they should

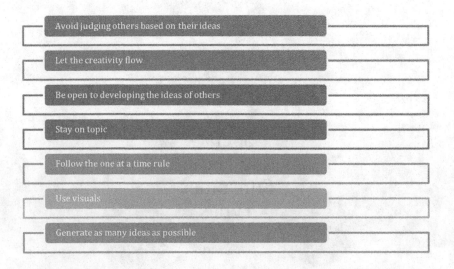

Figure 3.2 IDEO's Brainstorming Rules.
Source: https://www.ideou.com/blogs/inspiration/7-simple-rules-of-brainstorming.

choose the one's they assume would be most effective. In this phase, entrepreneurs may use techniques such as prototyping products and services or visiting makerspaces in order to develop a minimum viable product (MVP) that can be delivered to consumers.

A **minimum viable product** (MVP) is the most basic form of a product or service. The goal of initially creating the most basic or simple form of a product or service is that it allows entrepreneurs to "work out the kinks" in the product or service before they heavily invest in it emotionally and financially. Another goal is to use the MVP to test the market in an effort to learn more about consumer desires and thus be able to make improvements based on the knowledge gained from testing. A good example of an MVP used for these purposes is the iPhone. The first iPhone differs greatly from the iPhone 14 that exists today. The initial iPhone was the MVP, but as Apple learned more about what consumers needed, wanted, and what challenges they had using the phone, they updated it over time to have features that met their consumer needs.

Once an MVP is developed, entrepreneurs can test the ideas in the implementation phase. The implementation phase is about experimentation. One by one, the entrepreneur should test their solutions in order to validate their assumptions (the assumptions about what ideas would solve the problem). When they find a solution that works, they will achieve success by implementing it into their business model and delivering it to customers.

The process of human-centered design enables entrepreneurs to understand what needs they have that may be improved by a product or service. It takes into account their emotional and cultural realities through striving to empathize with the customer struggles and desires. For example, fashion retailers understand that while many people have clothing in their closets, they still have a desire to stay on top of the latest trends. Literally, their consumers don't need clothing, but they do need the feeling they get from obtaining new clothing that meets particular needs they have. Tools like the Design Thinking method and empathy mapping process may be used to facilitate this process.

Tools for Identifying and Assessing Consumer Needs

Empathy Map. An empathy map (shown in Figure 3.3) is a collaborative visualization tool that helps entrepreneurs explore and communicate what they know about a particular user of their products and services. It helps entrepreneurs make decisions about how to meet their consumer needs by asking and answering questions that aim to empathize with their needs. It can foster understanding of what drives a user's behavior.

Design Thinking. Design Thinking is a human-centered thinking process that deepens understanding about what drives user behavior and needs. As shown in Figure 3.4, it is a systematic process of collecting information on target or current users, outlining their issues, and then ideating and

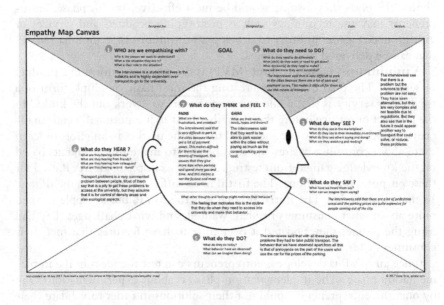

Figure 3.3 Empathy Map Canvas.

Source: https://medium.com/the-xplane-collection/updated-empathy-map-canvas-46df2 2df3c8a.

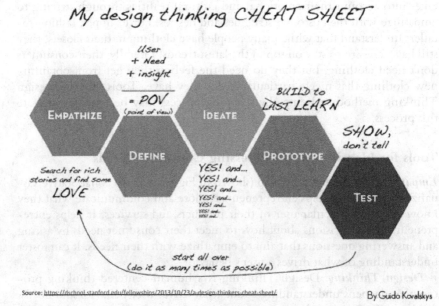

Figure 3.4 The Design Thinking Cheat Sheet.

prototyping solutions to their issues. The last stage of the Design Thinking process is to test solutions in the market to assess if user needs are adequately met. However, because consumers and the market change constantly, this process should be repeated as new products, services, and even policies need to be developed in an organization. Design Thinking is used by many companies, including Google, The Marriot, Lego, and IBM.

Social Needs for Social Impact

In the world of social entrepreneurship, social problems are an opportunity for social transformation. However, because social enterprises are organizations with dual goals (sometimes even triple), they attend to both needs that meet their social mission and goals that make them financially viable. Thus, while human-centered design focuses on understanding consumer needs from a business modeling perspective, the social mission that lies at the heart of social entrepreneurship requires a deep understanding of social needs and problems from the beneficiary perspective.

There are a variety of research methods that may help social entrepreneurs discover or expand their knowledge of the social problems they aim to address. Some examples include conducting case studies, reviewing research and news articles, focus groups, survey research, conducting stakeholder interviews, or engaging in participant observation of target beneficiaries to better understand their needs.

For example, one of the founders of Greyston Bakery volunteered with the homeless in order to learn more about their experiences, challenges, and needs. This form of participant observation helped him discover how barriers like not having an address and not having access to childcare prevent homeless people from obtaining the work needed for them to rise out of poverty. Greyston Bakery subsequently implemented an "open hiring policy" that hires anyone that applies for a job with their company. There is no job application or background check needed for employees. This policy enables Greyston Bakery to employ people who have challenges finding work, increasing their financial sustainability. In addition, Greyston Bakery provides daycare so their employees may go to work.

Understanding the social needs of your target beneficiaries enables social entrepreneurs to adequately create solutions that address them. Social needs are an opportunity for those needs to be fulfilled. Opportunity recognition is the ability to identify new goods, services, or raw materials that can be introduced into a market. Opportunities must be identified, developed, and evaluated. Figure 3.5 outlines various opportunities for social value creation, which is referred to as the *social value chain*. Within these opportunities, social needs may be directly or indirectly addressed. Many social enterprises have an indirect approach to social value creation. They may use the donation model, for example, to donate funds, resources, or materials to beneficiaries. On the other hand, many social enterprises run organizations that directly

| Procuring Supplies | Employing Workers | Designing the Product/ Service | Producing the Product / Service | Marketing to Target Customers |

Figure 3.5 The Simplified Social Value Chain.
Source: Dees, J. G., & Anderson, B. B. (2003). For-profit social ventures. *International Journal of Entrepreneurship Education*, 2(1), 1–26.

combine the social impact model and business model. For example, Blended Kitchen in Sheffield, England, runs a restaurant that mainly hires people from disadvantaged backgrounds in an effort to increase their financial self-sufficiency. Their employees are their beneficiaries, and they are interwoven into the business model because they operate the business.

Note: All of the opportunities in Figure 3.5 and more are outlined in Chapter 4 in detail.

While opportunity recognition is essential to organizational development, entrepreneurial capabilities are the ability to recognize a new opportunity and to develop the resources needed to pursue it. Anyone can come up with business ideas. Anyone can see a social need and develop a list of ways to address them. However, most people will not have the creativity, insight, and determination needed to take their ideas, and then acquire and organize resources in a way that transform the ideas into a social business model.

Bricolage (pronounced brick-o-lodge) is a popular term in some entrepreneurial circles. It involves making do with the resources at hand. There are three main components to bricolage, including:

1   <u>Making do</u> with the resources at hand by refusing to give in to limitations and combining resources for new or diverse purposes.
2   <u>Collecting "bits and pieces" of resources</u> that may come together in the future.
3   <u>Acquiring free or cheap resources</u>.

It is important to know that resources may be intellectual, human, financial, social, physical, cultural, political, or environmental (more on this in Chapter 4). Thus, social entrepreneurs using the mindset of bricolage would keep all of these types of resources in mind as they strive to develop their organizations.

Tools for Assessing Social Needs

Community Needs Assessment. A community needs assessment is a survey of issues, challenges, and/or desires in either a specific community of people or a particular geographic area. Community needs assessments are often project–specific in that they are surveys, questionnaires, or other methods that are specifically designed to assess the needs of a particular organization or community.

For the class, my students partnered with an organization called The Neighborhood Center that developed a Community Supported Agriculture (CSA) program that aimed to distribute fruits and vegetables at a low cost in the extremely impoverished community where it was located. While the program was running for months, there was a very small number of local residents who purchased produce from the program. Students in my class visited their facility and developed a community needs assessment to uncover why people were not taking advantage of this opportunity for produce when there were few places to purchase groceries in the city of approximately 77,000 people. They administered the survey to a total of 116 people in the community. Findings revealed that residents were unaware that the Neighborhood Center was an open and functioning facility. Thus, they never knew they had any programs at all because the façade of the facility was underdeveloped. There were also no signs or advertisements outside the facility or in the community that indicated that a CSA program was being offered at the center.

These findings substantially differ from the assumption that was made about the reasons why this problem arose, which was the idea that residents in the community did not like produce. This example highlights the importance of actually assessing community needs as opposed to making assumptions about them.

The Social Capability Intervention Model. The *Social Capability Intervention Model* (shown in Figure 3.6) is a model that I created after assessing the social, economic, and legal activities of 115 social enterprises across the United States. I examined the opportunities they create for beneficiaries through engaging in various activities and organized them by the following four overarching strategies for creating positive social change: (1) capacity building, (2) developing a social movement, (3) resource provision, and (4) systemic change.

Capacity building involves giving impoverished people, communities, or organizations tools and skills that enable them to help themselves. Respondents utilizing this technique emphasize training their beneficiaries to help themselves by equipping them with tools, knowledge, and skills. Developing a **social movement** consists of group action that aims to advance social change regarding one or more social issues by changing people's habits, thinking, or lifestyle. **Resource provision** is the provision of goods or services that help beneficiaries combat social issues. Social enterprises may provide resources for free or at an affordable cost to their beneficiaries. Lastly, **systemic change** involves advocating or working with governing institutions or elites in an effort to change the social systems that govern society.

The *Social Capability Intervention Model* is meant to be used in consulting and training programs to help guide aspiring and current social entrepreneurs in using their existing talents and skills to create social impact. For example, a social entrepreneur interested in improving the health and human security

Core Human Need Area	Health and Human Security	Social Mobility	Social, Political, and Environmental Engagement	Self-Expression and Social Relationships
Type of Social Capability	General Health Mental/emotional health Safety or abuse	Education Life-planning/decision-making Property ownership Employment training	Social issues and inclusion Discrimination issues Political participation Interaction with animals, plants, or nature	Independent/creative expression Recreation or entertainment
Capacity Building	Educating Training Counseling Coaching Financing Facility management	Educating Training Counseling Coaching Brokering and property management	Educating Training Counseling Coaching Gardening Farming Preserving nature	Educating Training Marketing
Social Movement	Convening Reducing pollution (land and water) Crowd sourcing	Convening Crowd sourcing	Convening Reducing pollution (land and water) Crowd sourcing	Convening Crowd sourcing
Resource Provision	Medical treatment Providing services or products Donations	Providing services or products Transitional Housing Donations	Providing services or products Donations	Manufacturing goods Event hosting Facility provision Providing services or products Donations
Systemic Change	Advocating for public policy development	Advocating for public policy development Providing or referring employment	Advocating for public policy development Developing a planned community Developing organizations	Providing employment
Target Beneficiaries	The general public Youth Businesses Homeowners Professionals Disadvantaged groups and communities The developing world	The general public Youth Farmers Schools Businesses Professionals Homeowners and tenants Social organizations Developers and architects Disadvantaged groups and communities Policy organizations	The general public Voters Youth Artists Farmers Specific geographic communities Businesses Professionals Disadvantaged groups	Youth Artists Professionals Disadvantaged groups and communities Specific geographic Communities Social organizations

(Left margin label: Activities by Strategy for Positive Social Change)

Figure 3.6 The Social Capability Intervention Model.
Source: Weaver, R. L. (2019). Social enterprise and the capability approach: Exploring how social enterprises are humanizing business. *Journal of Nonprofit and Public Sector Marketing*, 32, 427–452.

of a particular group of beneficiaries should explore their main strategy for positive social change. Once that is identified, they would consider the skills and talents in relation to the types of activities shown in the *Social Capability Intervention Model* to brainstorm ways they can design their social impact model and/or business model around their skills and interests. The model also outlines common beneficiaries for different core human need areas, but social entrepreneurs ultimately decide who their target beneficiaries are. The *Social Capability Intervention Model* is explained in both the online program and workbook designed to supplement this book.

Conclusion

When organizations continuously meet the needs of their consumers, their consumers continuously return. However, social enterprises desire more than just fulfilling the needs of their consumers, they strive to also meet the needs of their beneficiaries and other stakeholders. This desire is one of the qualities that distinguishes a social enterprise from a traditional commercial business and a traditional nonprofit organization. When social enterprises successfully fulfill this desire, they create both social impact and financial gain. However, it is of paramount importance to the long-term success of a social enterprise to understand that assessing consumer and social needs is a continuous and iterative process as opposed to a singular task. The market, people, and environment are always changing. In many ways we stay the same, yet we simultaneously change. The most successful organizations throughout history all understand these changes and thus invest in research that informs their ability to continuously adapt to them.

Case-In-Point: Design Thinking in Action

Author:
Robert Kissner
CEO of The Digital Arts Experience
Westchester, New York, United States

In mid-2015, Cisco Systems recognized that their HR practices, systems, and procedures were not working. Executive Vice President and Chief People, Policy & Purpose Officer, Francine Katsoudas, said that

> Our journey started with the realization that we in HR needed to show up [to work] differently. Work is changing faster than people, continuous transformation in the workplace is the norm, and the future of work requires people to think and work differently.[1]

In alignment with the growing involvement of Design Thinking and Innovation, Cisco acknowledged that a user-centric approach was necessary to solve their HR challenges because they position themselves a people-first company. Their employees are the biggest stakeholders in this equation, so a Human-Centered approach was a natural fit.

But rather than seek outside guidance of an HR-specific consultant or even a Design Thinking firm like IDEO, Cisco chose to look inward, to those whose insight about employee experiences would be most valuable, the employees themselves. Instead, they set out to completely disrupt HR at the company by organizing a 24-hour "break-a-thon," during which 800 employees across 39 countries worked together to create something entirely new. Cisco

> Launching an HR Hackathon provides a key message to all our HR people: pausing for 24 hours from the daily routine to team-up, think, work and have fun together – to make HR a better place for our employees and for ourselves.[2]

What resulted was over 100 ideas spanning various HR areas, including onboarding, PTO, leadership, workplace design, and more. The ideas were presented and several winners were chosen, including a complete overhaul of the onboarding process for new employees that involves a mobile app designed to help new hires navigate their first weeks on the job (Figure 3.7).

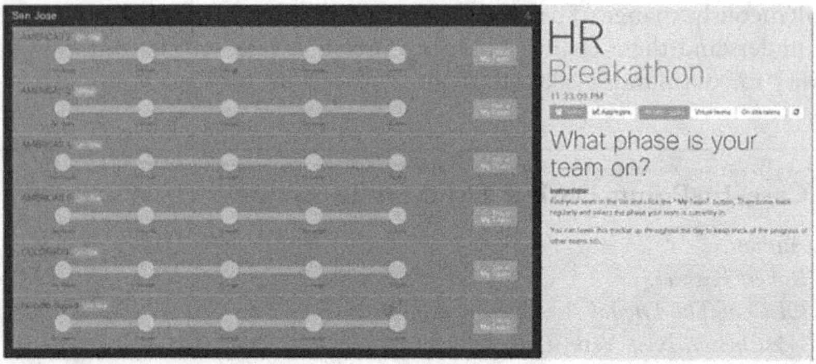

Figure 3.7 HR Breakathon.

This entire act, stopping operations for 800 employees, asking them to identify the issues that they face, and giving them the time, resources, and ownership to create solutions, signaled to the entire company that the leadership recognizes them as their most valuable resource and that they truly care about their needs. What's more is the act of looking internally versus bringing in an outside consulting firm doubles down their people-first message.

This case clearly demonstrates the power of a user-first approach in a corporate setting, but consider the impact in the setting of developing a social enterprise. Looking at the Double Diamond of Design Thinking, a problem is defined and understood by an entrepreneur via talking with users and understanding their perspective on the issue. A potential solution is then tested by involving users and collecting their feedback via a User Feedback Grid. A common misconception is that between those actions, the entrepreneur "returns to the office" and hits the drawing board to brainstorm and prototype a solution before bringing it to the users for testing. Rephrased, this process could be described as designing for the users (Figures 3.8 and 3.9).

While this is an effective way to apply Design Thinking, consider instead that the social entrepreneur designs **with** their users. Rather than "returning to the office," the entrepreneur asks the community to participate in the entire process, to involve them in the brainstorming process, and to participate in the development of prototypes. Imagine the impact of constantly bringing in key stakeholders from the community to brainstorm new ideas or share progress on prototypes. This action not only facilitates the development of solutions that truly meet the needs of the community but clearly communicates that the entrepreneur is invested in the community and not simply looking to capitalize on their needs. Designing with users establishes trust, builds relationships, and creates confidence in the product or service.

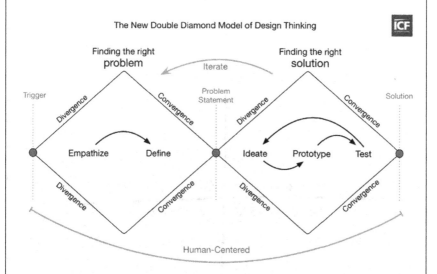

Figure 3.8 The New Double Diamond Model of Design Thinking.
Source: https://medium.com/good-design/visualizing-the-4-essentials-of-design-thinking-17fe5c191c22.

A great example of this is SELCO, a solar energy company in India. After suffering significant financial hardship due to premature attempts at growth and a spike in the cost of solar components, Harish Hande, the founder of SELCO, doubled down on his missions of supporting India's poor and sought out investors who aligned with his vision. His first action was to embark on an extensive needs assessment. Spending time with midwives, street vendors, or rural farmers, SELCO determined each group's needs and altered off-the-shelf solar equipment as needed to align with their unique needs for electricity and lighting. He installed lights personally in various villages and built teams of local technicians from rural areas to maintain equipment, eventually growing the team to over 500 employees.[3,4]

Hande's actions of spending time with his users to understand their needs, personally working in rural areas to install equipment, and involving his stakeholders in the solution by employing them to install and maintain equipment communicated that their needs were his top priority. These actions made it clear that he is not a hotshot entrepreneur trying to take advantage of the poor but someone who they could trust.

There are countless other successful social enterprises that demonstrate the importance of this user-first approach to doing business. Thrive Farmers, The Embrace Warmer, Uncommon Goods, and Project Masiluleke are just a few examples of successful ventures that

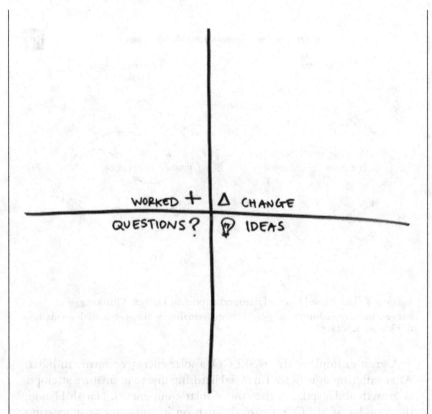

Figure 3.9 Feedback Grid.
Source: https://www.ibm.com/design/thinking/page/toolkit/activity/feedback-grid.

maintained a mission-driven, user-first approach to doing business, and the impact of this mindset is clear in both their success as businesses and their impact on the communities that they serve.

Design Thinking is a powerful and relevant tool in entrepreneurship. Regardless of whether it is applied in an international corporation or a small social enterprise, the Design Thinking mindset puts users first in order to create great solutions. For social entrepreneurs, the idea of designing with the community versus designing for the community takes Design Thinking a step further. Involving the community from day one, throughout the Design Thinking process, and on an ongoing basis provides empowerment to stakeholders, builds trust, and clearly communicates the social entrepreneur's commitment to their needs.

Notes

1 https://www.shrm.org/resourcesandtools/hr-topics/organizational-and-employee-development/pages/cisco-changed-hr-in-24-hours-using-design-thinking.aspx.
2 ciscoglobalhrbreakathonfeb2016-160404103637.pdf.
3 https://www.sustainablejungle.com/sustainable-tech/selco-india-social-business/.
4 https://vol10.cases.som.yale.edu/selco/overview/introduction.

4 Social Enterprise and Community Development

I honestly feel that if we filled every poor community in the world with social enterprises, that sought to identify and alleviate their community's most pressing needs, it would be a game changer... a world changer. My life's work examines how social enterprises may be utilized as a tool for advancing community and economic development. Social enterprises are a medium through which social problems are transformed into opportunities for positive social change. However, a student of mine once asked me "what makes a social enterprise 'social?'" She then went on to explain that there are social groups that band together over negative, money-making activities like gangs, the mafia, or even organizations that promote racism and gun violence. What is the difference between a social enterprise and groups that develop organizations around a legal social activity that may not necessarily be morally or ethically sound? The question was simple, but brilliant. It made me start adding the word "positive" before the term social change. In reality, social change can indeed be positive or negative.

True **community development**, however, must be positive. Community development may be defined as the process of creating and increasing solidarity and agency. **Solidarity** is a deeply shared identity and code of conduct. **Conflicting** ideas and visions are a natural part of community development and must be sorted through to build solidarity. **Agency** is about building the capacity for people to understand, create, act, and reflect. Community developers build capacity of others when they encourage or teach people to create their own dreams and learn new skills and knowledge. We can distinguish social enterprises from other social organizations that engage in questionable behavior by formally and informally requiring them to be ethically and morally sound. Engaging in activities that harm society, all or specific groups of people, and/or the environment is not ethically and morally sound. It does not contribute to positive social change or community development.

In this chapter, we explore the role of social enterprise in community development while recognizing that the term community can refer to a shared place or even a shared idea among people and organizations that has no geographic boundary. Social enterprises may view their communities based on a particular geographic boundary that they seek to improve. They may also see their community as people who share the same passion for a social issue that

DOI: 10.4324/9781003226963-5

they strive to combat. Regardless of whether a social enterprise has a place-based or issue-based sense of community, it has a reciprocal relationship with that community. This reciprocal relationship involves both giving to that community and receiving a diversity of resources from that community. This chapter explains this relationship and outlines the community capitals that advance social enterprise and community development.

Defining Community and the Importance of Context

Community development takes time. Most societal issues that we see and experience today are not newly developed problems. They are the result of years, decades, and even centuries of abuse in some form. Poverty, racism, gender discrimination, the abuse faced by the LGBTQ community, climate change, homelessness, and other issues have been with us for quite some time. However, that fact should not discourage you at all. All progress takes time and thus any progress should be celebrated. As a black female of Jamaican and Cuban descent who was born and raised in the Bronx, New York, I know that racism exists today. However, I am also aware that through much progress in laws, education, and anti-racist interventions that I was born and raised in a world that is kinder and freer than that of my parents let alone my ancestors.

In the wise words of American Civil Rights Activist Audre Lorde, "Revolution is not a one-time event." Community development is an ongoing process that evolves over time as the needs of communities and beneficiaries evolve. So, while many issues exist today that have existed for centuries, in many cases, the improvements that have been made have reflectively left us in a better place. The work that today's social entrepreneurs do, if effective, will also advance community development in its own right.

Place-Based and Issue-Based Community Development

With all that said, community development may be place-based or issue-based. Place-based factors may help or hinder the emergence of social enterprise, as they are influenced by a social enterprise's social mission, revenue generation models, and legal structure.

The term **embeddedness** refers to the process of social enterprises immersing themselves into a community in an effort to understand and use local resources and rules to create value. Embeddedness enables social enterprises to anchor themselves within a community. However, over-embeddedness can stifle institutional changes because of deviance from community norms (e.g. group think). In such cases, disembedding may be necessary for a social enterprise to evolve.

Social enterprises that have a place-based focus often develop to meet the needs of their local community. As mentioned in Chapter 1 of this book, many people become social entrepreneurs because they have direct experience with the problem they aim to address. In many cases, either they have experienced or witnessed someone they care for deal with a social problem and decided to take action to combat it. Because of this individual experience, there is often a local focus on addressing local needs. However, local community needs change throughout time. Many place-based social enterprises start from small beginnings, but as they deepen their understanding of community needs over time, they grow in a variety of ways (e.g. number of beneficiaries served, types of services offered, revenue sources). For place-based social enterprises, their work is viewed as an investment in their community. Their relationship with their community is often reciprocal.

While some social enterprises view community from a place-based perspective, others define community around one or more particular social issues. Their work may be based in a particular geographic area, but may extend to national and global audiences. For example, Grameen Bank is a social enterprise that started in Bangladesh but their mission inspires social enterprises globally. Social enterprises with an issue-based sense of community benefit from a global network of collaborators, resources, and opportunities. However, that takes time to establish and usually starts locally in the beginning.

Reciprocal Relationships with Your Community

In an ideal world, all organizations would strive to develop reciprocal relationships with their local communities. While this is not the case for all organizations, it is critical that social enterprises aim to develop reciprocal relationships with their communities and stakeholders over time. Social enterprises produce goods, services, and/or programs that benefit their communities, but may also obtain community-based resources such as volunteers, unused space, donated goods, financial assets, professional skills, customer loyalty, locally produced goods, and more.

Reciprocal relationships may be developed through reaching out to power players and leaders in a community. Reaching out to community members, communicating your goals to them, and listening to their goals in order to identify parallel interests may facilitate connections that strengthen over time. If power players do not know you exist, they cannot help you nor can you truly help them (recall the importance of assessing needs) (Figure 4.1).

Social enterprise activities can have various social, environmental, cultural, and financial benefits on their local community. The United Kingdom, for example, has designated some neighborhoods as "Registered Social Enterprise Places." These areas are places where social enterprise activities are thriving. They bring together residents, educational institutions, government, and businesses to create a culture of social entrepreneurship.

Productive Opportunity Space

A productive opportunity space is a space within the market where there is a (1) valuable product or service to be delivered, (2) a motivated actor to

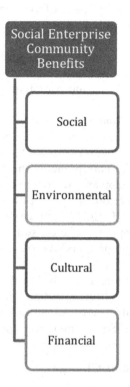

Figure 4.1 Social Enterprise Community Benefits.

deliver it, and (3) the availability of resources needed to fulfill the opportunity. Social entrepreneurs see community needs as opportunity spaces, but not all opportunities are productive. Let's explore why the convergence of these factors are important.

1   ***The recognition of a valuable service*** – Everyone has ideas, but not all ideas are valuable or profitable. Many aspiring entrepreneurs develop their ideas individually without seeking out knowledge about their target consumer. Yet, if they want to develop a sustainable organization, they must learn to attend to consumer needs, as highlighted in Chapter 3. When an entrepreneur identifies a genuine need among consumers that they or another party find valuable enough to pay for, they have identified a valuable service.

2   ***The identification of a motivated actor to act on the opportunity*** – Just like anyone can have an idea, anyone can have a business idea. However, it takes a resilient, passionate, determined, risk-taking, and adaptive person to be an entrepreneur. Why? Because entrepreneurship of any kind is hard. Failure is a large part of entrepreneurship. Social entrepreneurs

may fail to hire the right people, fail to design the right startup business model, fail to collaborate, fail to attract customers, and so on and so on. It takes a tenacious spirit to have the courage to pitch a business idea (especially a socially conscious business idea) to the world and dare to make it a reality. There are many people who are brilliant, creative, and innovative, but still lack the motivation and resilience needed to be an entrepreneur.

3   *The knowledge of available resources* – Entrepreneurs, as motivated actors, should seek out financial and non-financial resources that may bring their venture to life. However, it is not enough to merely identify and secure resources. Social entrepreneurs should seek guidance on *how to utilize* resources to develop an effective and efficient cost-saving business model. In addition, developing a good business model and plan helps social entrepreneurs identify the key activities needed to deliver their goods and services (value proposition) to consumers. Once outlined, social entrepreneurs can seek out partners who may provide the resources needed to bring their venture to life.

4   The process of identifying a valuable product or service, being a motivated enough actor to deliver it, and seeking out and securing available resources needed to fulfill an opportunity is what encompasses a productive opportunity space. Social enterprises thrive in such spaces.

Theory of Positive Social Change

While the productive opportunity space helps social entrepreneurs identify valuable services and resources, the theory of positive social change (in social entrepreneurship) is an explanation for *how* a social entrepreneur or organization plans to transform a social problem into a solution. The solution consists of positive outcomes. In my research on social enterprises, I have identified four overarching strategies that social enterprises employ to advance positive social change, including capacity building, advancing a social movement, resource provision, and systemic change.

Capacity building involves giving impoverished people, communities, or organizations tools and skills that enable them to help themselves. Social enterprises that use this technique create opportunities for their beneficiaries that involve "self-help," which essentially refers to giving them the tools to help themselves (e.g. employment opportunities, specialized educational training).

Developing a *social movement* consists of group action that aims to advance social change regarding one or more social issues by changing people's habits, thinking, or lifestyle.

Resource provision is the provision of goods, services, or resources that may help beneficiaries combat social issues or meet their needs. Social enterprises may provide resources (e.g. medical supplies) for free or at an affordable cost to their beneficiaries.

Lastly, **systemic change** involves advocating or working with governing institutions or elites in an effort to change the social systems that govern society. Systemic change can also apply to developing new organizations or communities that foster community-wide changes.

Community Capitals

One question I ask when evaluating the efficacy of a social enterprise intervention is "what is this organization's capacity for stimulating positive social change or hindering negative social change?" The answer, in part, lies within the community capitals that the social enterprise possesses or has the potential to acquire. Community capitals are resources and characteristics that aid in a community's ability to grow and prosper. Many aspiring and early stage social entrepreneurs discuss startup funding at great length when designing and trying to launch their organizations. However, financial capital is only one form of community capital. Table 4.1 outlines eight different types of community capital, along with examples of each type. A social entrepreneur who identifies and understands the community capitals in their community may utilize them to establish, build, and grow their business.

As a scholar with a passion for advancing community development, I would be remiss if I wrote a book about creating sustainable social enterprises without the importance of community capitals. Recall the social enterprise ecosystem map in Chapter 2. The map in this chapter (Figure 4.2) is complete with examples of factors that make up a social enterprise ecosystem. This one, however, is blank. In my workshops, I use the blank map to guide social entrepreneurs to study their own geographic ecosystem and the community capitals that lie within it. In a way, community capitals reflect the idea that opportunity is all around you. They are a holistic view of community resources.

Human capital is one of the most essential components of any organization. It is the people power that drives operations. It may be defined as the skills, knowledge, experience, and even health possessed by individuals or a population of people. Numerous studies have found that communities with high levels of human capital tend to have high levels of entrepreneurship and success overall. The smarter and healthier a population of people are, the more successful and innovative they usually are.

Physical capital, from a community development perspective, is comprised of the buildings and infrastructure that make up a community. Within an organization, it may also refer to equipment or objects that help produce its goods and services. The importance of physical capital often changes throughout one's entrepreneurial journey. For example, the famous burger chain Shake Shack was first established as a food cart located in Madison Square Park in Manhattan. As its customer base grew, it developed a very small restaurant in the park that sold fries, a burger, and lemonade. I frequented the restaurant in college so I remember the long lines that wrapped

Table 4.1 Examples of Community Capitals

Human Capital	Social Capital
- Employees - Contractors - Partners - Interns - Advisors/mentors - Educational opportunities or incentives - Professional development	- Trust - Leadership - Networks - Reciprocal relationships in a community or with people in power
Physical Capital	**Intellectual Capital**
- Buildings - Office space - Equipment - Computers, laptops, phones - Vehicles - Land	- Databases - Publications - Trade secrets - Patents - Trademarks - Technology - Intellectual property
Economic Capital	**Natural Capital**
- Grants - Loans (low to no interest) - Credit lines - Seed-funding - Community development banks - Credit unions - Venture capital funds - Microenterprise loan funds - Angel investors	- Weather - Geographic location - Natural resources - Natural beauty - Local flora and fauna
Cultural Capital	**Political Capital**
- Language - Rituals - Traditions - Symbols - Dress - Crops/food	- Inclusion/exclusion - Voice - Power - Resources

around the park well. However, now that Shake Shack has solidified their business model, the company has scaled. It now has dozens of locations all around the world. Their need for physical capital was small in the startup phase, but it grew substantially as their business grew, which is common throughout the entrepreneurial journey.

Economic capital includes economic resources like cash, credit, investments, and property. It strongly contributes to organizational sustainability. One of the biggest challenges that social enterprises face relates to cash flow management. Thus, identifying diverse funding opportunities may substantially contribute to social enterprise development and growth.

Capital Infrastructure

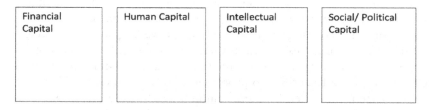

| Financial Capital | Human Capital | Intellectual Capital | Social/ Political Capital |

Social Enterprises -> Beneficiaries Served -> Positive Social Impact

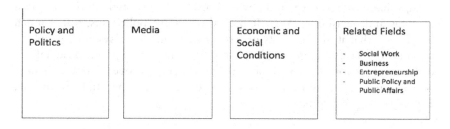

| Policy and Politics | Media | Economic and Social Conditions | Related Fields |

Related Fields:
- Social Work
- Business
- Entrepreneurship
- Public Policy and Public Affairs

Context Setting Factors

Figure 4.2 Social Enterprise Ecosystem Map.
Note: All community capitals are not provided on the ecosystem map. Entrepreneurs should tailor the map to their needs.

Social capital consists of the relationships we have with people who have power and resources. In social entrepreneurship, social capital is comprised of the entrepreneur's professional and personal network. It also includes opportunities that exist in a given community to expand an entrepreneur's network.

Intellectual capital consists of ideas, knowledge, skills, and even intellectual property that foster wealth and opportunity. Intellectual capital is often intangible because of its intellectual nature, but it may also come in the form of databases and email lists that can substantially contribute to the development of an institution. One example of an intangible form of intellectual capital is a trade secret, which is a type of intellectual property often used in business that is kept secret (e.g. recipe to Coca Cola soda) so the business may retain its competitive advantage.

Natural capital is comprised of natural resources like the ocean, soils, vegetation, water, minerals, and living organisms. Communities with high levels of natural capital may find entrepreneurial opportunities in them. For example, Dunn's River Falls in Ocho Rios, Jamaica, is one of many beautiful natural waterfalls on the island. A once public resource, visitors must now pay to visit and climb Dunn's River Falls. There are strengths and weaknesses to transforming natural resources into entrepreneurial opportunities; however, Dunn's River Falls is one of many examples of how that may be done.

Cultural capital involves the social assets that people feature including the way they speak, dress, style their hair, values, behaviors, and even their ownership patterns. Community developers often have to gain trust in order to influence community leaders. In this respect, having and understanding the importance of cultural capital is important for also building social capital. Cultural capital influences who people feel comfortable with and thus willing to welcome into their lives and communities. Social entrepreneurs seeking to embed themselves into communities would do well to increase their cultural capital within that community.

Political capital is the ability to influence and control individuals and groups that have resources and power. It involves the potential to gain access to elites and decision-makers. It may also involve politicians, but is much broader in that it also consists of having influence over systems, people, a community. Trust and goodwill are important factors in political capital because in order for an entrepreneur to have influence over people, policies, or a community, they must trust you to deliver on some kind of promise, expectation, or outcome.

Conclusion

Social enterprises are a medium through which social services are delivered to people that need them. They do this through revenue-generation techniques and leveraging different community capitals. In social entrepreneurship, community may be defined geographically or by issue/social cause. While a place-based community focuses on a particular geographic area, an issue-based community revolves around a common desire to address social issues. This desire is shared across space and time. Embeddedness involves immersing a social enterprise into the local culture, regulatory systems, and economic climate of a community and utilizing assets within that community. It aids in an organization's ability to discover and access different community capitals. However, a social enterprise should never be so embedded within a community that group think begins to occur and thus stifles development of the organization.

5 Models of Social Impact

The most frequently asked question I am asked about social enterprises is how can a business or organization create social impact? Should they just donate money to a social cause? Should they run a for-profit business that donates money to charity like Newman's Own? This chapter is all about answering such questions. The commonality among all social enterprises is their drive to intentionally address social problems. However, social enterprises may have one or more social impact model(s) that guide the activities they engage in to create positive social change. A **social impact model** is a strategy or model that a social enterprise uses to solve or address a social problem. This chapter outlines ten common social impact models and provides illustrative case studies for each to show how these models work in action.

Donation Model

This model focuses on donating financial, time, or physical resources to people in need or organizations that help disadvantaged people and communities. The donation model has been made popular by organizations such as Newman's Own that donate all of their profits to charity and eyewear company Warby Parker that donates a pair of glasses for each pair purchased. This model is relatively easy to get started. Entrepreneurs use the donation model by donating profits or products to people or communities in need or the organizations that support them. These donations can be continuous or occasional. This ease is likely why it's so popular. Entrepreneurs who use this model often are not directly involved with the cause or charitable activity, leaving them time to focus on running their organizations. As such, it may be a great starting point for social entrepreneurial activity.

Social Hiring

Social hiring is intentionally hiring people who face challenges to obtaining employment such as people who are formerly incarcerated, homeless, the mentally or physically disabled, people who have low educational attainment, and undocumented workers. Depending on the region of the world, social

DOI: 10.4324/9781003226963-6

Cases

TOMS Shoes Los Angeles, USA	Newman's Own Connecticut, USA	I AM More Scarsdale Westchester, USA
Donates a pair of shoes to people in need for every pair of shoes purchased.	Donates all profits to their own charity, the Newman's Own Foundation. The foundation then distributes the funds to various charities and social causes.	I AM More Scarsdale is a clothing boutique in Scarsdale, New York. It offers a luxury clothing and lifestyle collection called "The Strong and Beautiful collection" that donates a portion of all sales to a nonprofit organization called Safe Horizon. Safe Horizon helps victims of domestic violence, child abuse, sexual abuse, and human trafficking.

enterprises that use this model may be called work integration social enterprises, affirmative businesses, social firms, or employment social enterprises. Social hiring aims to grant opportunities for economic self-sufficiency among society's most vulnerable populations and it works! Research has found that social hiring can:

- Reduce the re-entry rate of people who were formerly incarcerated
- Reduce substance abuse
- Reduce reliance on public assistance
- Help beneficiaries obtain and sustain housing
- Increase their professional and social network

Like the donation model, social hiring is also relatively popular in the social enterprise sector. However, as described above, it can be a much more in-depth and impactful experience for beneficiaries.

Cases

Homeboy Industries California, USA	Kings Kitchen North Carolina, USA
Homeboy Industries provides employment, healing, substance abuse, social support, and other training opportunities for former gang members and people who were formerly incarcerated in order to help them live fulfilling lives.	Kings Kitchen is a gourmet southern food restaurant that intentionally hires people who were formerly incarcerated, homeless, or who struggle with substance abuse.

Capability Building/Training

Capacity building involves giving impoverished people, communities, or organizations the tools and skills that enable them to help themselves. In my research, social entrepreneurs who use this technique emphasize creating "self-help" opportunities for their beneficiaries, essentially offering skills and opportunities to help themselves today and in the long-run (e.g. employment opportunities, specialized educational training). Examples of this may include providing training to people from vulnerable backgrounds and/or equipping people to run social enterprises or social programs.

Capacity building social enterprise models come in various forms. Some entrepreneurs create transitional housing programs that house the homeless, but have some kind of employment until they are able to economically sustain themselves. Other programs may offer professional development training like goal-setting, budgeting, and interviewing workshops to people who lack such skills. The primary idea behind these initiatives is, as the old saying goes, to teach a person to fish so you can feed them for life instead of giving them a fish to feed them for a day.

Cases		
Women's Bean Project Colorado, USA	Venice on Vine Ohio, USA	Stroopies Lancaster, Pennsylvania, USA
Women's Bean Project helps low-income and disadvantaged women advance in life by offering professional development training, job opportunities, and networking opportunities.	Venice on Vine is a pizzeria and catering kitchen that offers employment training and job placement to people who have trouble finding employment.	Stroopies is a baked goods shop that hires refugee women in order to help them create new lives in Lancaster. Their hiring process is focused on transitional hiring, meaning they aim to help refugees acclimate to the community before they move on to more advanced employment.

Social Service or Resource Provision

Resource provision is the delivery or offering of goods, services, or resources that may help beneficiaries combat social issues or meet their needs. Social enterprises provide resources (e.g., medical supplies) for free or at an affordable cost to their beneficiaries. Many social enterprises engage in social service or resource provision and there are various, intriguing models for such work. In addition, this model often combines other social impact models as you will see in the case studies below.

Some social enterprises choose to operate as a "medium" for the alleviation of social problems in a particular community. In this sense, the organization studies and identifies social issues in a community and then develops interventions that aim to reduce or eradicate the issues. Resource provision may also look different. During the COVID-19 pandemic, a social enterprise called A Safe Haven in Chicago, Illinois, created an alternative housing option for people who tested positive for the coronavirus, a highly transmittable and deadly virus. By providing housing for COVID-19-positive community members, A Safe Haven helped stop the spread of the virus in their community. In fall 2020, they won the city of Chicago's Innovation Award for their work.

Cases

A Safe Haven *Chicago, Illinois, USA*	*Aspen Pointe and Aspen Pointe Cafe* *Colorado Springs, Colorado, USA*
A Safe Haven offers a variety of social programs related to developing the mental, employment, social, and economic standing of people in need. Offerings include transitional housing for the homeless, youth skill building programs, job training programs, and behavioral health programs.	Aspen Pointe offers a variety of social services aimed at improving human well-being such as individual and group therapy, literacy, post-secondary educational training, childcare services, and career planning.

Social Procurement

Social procurement is the acquisition of a range of assets and services, with the aim of intentionally creating social outcomes (both directly and indirectly). Essentially, it involves people, organizations, and governments "buying good." Social procurement is popular throughout Australia, the United Kingdom, and Canada, but it is also slowly growing in the United States. In the United States, there are policies like the Javits-Wagner O' Day Act (now the AbilityOne program) that require the government to purchase from organizations that employ people with disabilities. This policy is a great step, but more work needs to be done to create opportunities for social procurement at the regional and national level in the United States. However, Australia and Canada both have strong networks of social procurement-focused organizations pioneered by institutions like Social Traders in Australia and Buy Social Canada. Both Social Traders and Buy Social Canada work with local and regional governments to broker social purchasing relationships between government, businesses, and social enterprises. Their work has led to millions of dollars in contracts related to "buying social."

Cases

Procurement of Social Services	Procurement of Public Works	Allocation of a Percentage of Work to a Social Enterprise	Corporate Social Responsibility
Social Traders	City of Vancouver via Buy Social Canada	AbilityOne Program	Vermont Business for Social Responsibility (VBSR)
A number of for-profit companies in Australia work with Social Traders to connect them to social enterprises that hire people from marginalized and disadvantaged backgrounds. Through these contracts, they amplify the delivery of a diversity of social services to their primary beneficiaries.	Buy Social Canada works with and recommends policy related to advancing funding for social procurement contracts for social enterprises in Vancouver. These contracts focus on creating social purchasing opportunities between the city and develop benefit agreements.	The AbilityOne program in the United States creates employment opportunities and trains people with disabilities such as blindness and deafness to join the workforce. The program enables federal organizations to directly purchase supplies from organizations that hire people with disabilities.	VBSR is based in the city of Burlington, Vermont, and works with for-profit companies that want to engage in social good. The companies do not take a stance to become social enterprises, but they work with VBSR to become more socially conscious in terms of employee treatment and wages, impact on the environment, and more.

There are four main types of social procurement initiatives, including:

1 Procurement of Social Services – The acquisition of goods or services directly from socially conscious organizations (e.g. social enterprises, nonprofit organizations).

2 Procurement of Public Works – The intentional purchase of a particular outcome for public good, usually purchased from a private business. Examples include the construction of hospitals, schools, churches, playgrounds, parks, etc.

3 Allocation of a Percentage of Work to a Social Enterprise – When a contract is issued to have a particular package of work or service completed by a social enterprise.

4 Corporate Social Responsibility (Management of Supply Chains) – The desire to procure from socially conscious organizations, usually by for-profit businesses, that do not cause social or environmental harm.

Definition Source: Furneaux, C., & Barraket, J. (2014). Purchasing social good (s): A definition and typology of social procurement. *Public Money & Management, 34*(4), 265–272.

Selling Socially Conscious Products or Services

Goods or services that are themselves a benefit to the person using them or that help alleviate a social problem. Examples of such goods or services include organic foods, selling medical equipment at an affordable cost, or upcycling services that reduce waste and pollution. Many of these goods require educating social enterprise consumers and beneficiaries on what makes these products or services beneficial. For example, eating foods with gluten are commonplace in society. However, in recent years, there has been a growing body of research indicating that gluten may create or exacerbate health issues in some people. While some may see eating gluten-free products as a fad, others may genuinely receive health and wellness benefits by consuming such products. However, they must first be educated to understand the reasons why such products may be beneficial to them.

Cases	
Adore Boutique *Michigan, USA*	*Seventh Generation* *Burlington, Vermont, USA*
Adore Boutique is a sustainable fashion boutique that sells women apparel and accessories that was produced in a socially responsible and safe manner. Many of the brands sold in the store are run by women from disadvantaged backgrounds around the world. The boutique donates 15% of profits to organizations that fight sex trafficking.	Seventh Generation sells environmentally friendly products such as household cleaning items, childcare products, and feminine care products. The business also has a foundation that provides grants to environmentally friendly charities.

Social Marketing

Advertising techniques or campaigns that aim to spread awareness about social problems and/or ways to address social issues. In recent years, a growing number of social movements and protests have erupted around the world, due to growing inequalities related to income, race, gender, religion, and more. Some social enterprises aim to combat these issues by directly creating marketing campaigns, products, and informational workshops that aim to educate and inspire others to take action.

Cases

Ben and Jerry's Ice Cream *Vermont, USA*	*Buy Social* *(Various Locations Around the World)*
Ben and Jerry's is a well-known ice cream company that has a social mission. While the company engages in a variety of socially beneficial activities, they are known for their social marketing strategies that shed light on social issues like the Black Lives Matter movement, war, poverty, and more. From creating honest and critical social media campaigns to dedicating ice cream flavors to social causes, Ben and Jerry's is one the first companies in the world to place a social mission in equal importance to its product and economic missions.	Buy Social programs or campaigns differ around the world, but what they all have in common is that they promote and sometimes facilitate the importance of consumer and institutional buying from social enterprises. Buy Social Canada, for example, coordinates institutional and government purchasing from social enterprises to boost their impact. Buy Social Jamaica is a platform that promotes the work of social enterprises in Jamaica to encourage people to purchase from them.

Systemic Change

Systemic change involves advocating or working with governing institutions and/or elites in an effort to change the social systems that govern society. It can encompass developing new organizations, planned communities, or even working to develop new public policies that foster community-wide changes. Social enterprises using a model of systemic change recognize that while working with beneficiaries is important, it is also important to build relationships and form initiatives with people in powerful positions related to the main issues they seek to combat. This model is particularly appropriate for addressing deep-rooted issues like racism, poverty, criminal justice, and environmental degradation.

Cases

Social Enterprise Greenhouse *Rhode Island, USA*	*Zero Waste Event Productions* *Ohio, USA*
Social Enterprise Greenhouse works to create and scale businesses that aim to address social issues in Rhode Island and beyond. Social Enterprise Greenhouse runs a variety of business training and networking programs that are changing what it means to be a business. In addition, they foster systemic change by working with legislators and institutional partners to push federal and state legislation related to social enterprise like the Benefit Corporation legislation.	Zero Waste Event Productions reuses, recycles, and composts waste products that result from large events and festivals. Their goal is to reduce waste and pollution that end up in landfills in an effort to create a more sustainable world.

Social Movement

Developing a social movement consists of group action that aims to advance social change regarding one or more social issues by changing people's habits, thinking, or lifestyle. Social movements often involve convening people from different socioeconomic and cultural backgrounds to explore, educate, and discuss a problem in an effort to address ways to alleviate it. However, it may also simply involve informing people of social issues.

Cases

Cancer Research UK United Kingdom	The Peace and Justice Center Burlington, Vermont, USA
Cancer Research UK is an organization that runs thrift shops and engages in other commercial activities that spread awareness about cancer causes, alleviation, and research. Funds generated from commercial activities are used to support cancer treatment and research initiatives.	Vermont is one of the least diverse states in the United States. However, the Peace and Justice Center in Burlington, Vermont, aims to eradicate racism by hosting anti-racist skill building workshops and spreading awareness about toxic behaviors that contribute to racism. It funds its services partly through its store that sells arts, crafts, and educational materials created by people from diverse and disadvantaged backgrounds.

Social Finance Services or Products

Social finance services and products are goods, services, or initiatives that aim to improve economic self-sufficiency or attend to the financial challenges of disadvantaged groups or people of different levels of socioeconomic status. This social impact model is broad, as it includes initiatives such as developing microfinance organizations, impact investing, crowdsourcing the financing of social organizations or programs, offering tiered rates for products, and awarding restricted grants for marginalized communities.

Cases

Grameen Bank Dhaka, Bangladesh	Community Sourced Capital (now transformed into the People's Economy Lab) Seattle, United States
Grameen Bank is a bank based in Bangladesh, founded by Muhammad Yunus. The bank offers small loans to poverty-stricken people that enables them to create small businesses and build modest houses to live in. In traditional bank systems, giving loans to people who don't have a form of security (assets including land, consistent income, etc.) was rare, and if loans were approved, they were accompanied by exuberant interest rates, which set disadvantaged people back further. Yunus disrupted the cycle by personally lending $27 to 42 women from the village of Jobra. Each of the women repaid their loan. The women he helped invested in their own capacity for generating income and improving their economic standing.	Community Sourced Capital was an organization in Seattle, Washington, that organized local residents to invest money into developing local businesses that address local needs. Once the businesses were operating, they would pay the loan back without interest. While Community Sourced Capital is no longer in operation, its model is a great example of a targeted crowdfunding campaign. In its place, its leaders now run the People's Economy Lab, an organization that aims to systematically address economic inequality in Seattle.

Each of these social impact models is a strategy that social enterprises use to create positive social change. There may be overlap between models, especially as social enterprises evolve over time. Social enterprises have been found to adopt more social impact strategies as their revenue increases. In addition, some social enterprises start with one model in mind, but incorporate or switch models over time to better attend to their target beneficiaries. For this reason, I always recommend adopting a "learn as we go" mentality in entrepreneurship. What works for an entrepreneur in one phase of business may not work in another. Flexibility and openness is critical to successful entrepreneurship, whether social or commercial (Table 5.1).

Table 5.1 Social Impact Models

Social Impact Models	Examples
Donation model	TOMS Shoes in Los Angeles, California, USA
	Newman's Own in Westport, Connecticut, USA
	Sweet Charity in Vergennes, Vermont, USA
Social hiring	Deaf Can Coffee in Kingston, Jamaica
	Inspiration Kitchen in Chicago, Illinois, USA
	Blend Kitchen in Sheffield, England
	CK Cafe in Camden, New Jersey, USA
	Homeboy Industries in Los Angeles, California, USA
	Stroopies in Lancaster, Pennsylvania, USA
	Greyston Bakery in Yonkers, New York, USA
Capacity building/ training	AspenPointe in Colorado Springs, Colorado, USA
	Kuli Kuli in Oakland, California, USA
	Women's Bean Project in Denver, Colorado, USA
Social service or resource provision	Seventh Generation in Burlington, Vermont, USA
	ReSource in Burlington, Vermont, USA
	DoorDash Social Impact Team in New York, New York, USA
Social procurement	Numerous organizations engage in such work. Organizations that facilitate this process include:
	– Buy Social Canada in Vancouver, Canada
	– Social Traders in Melbourne, Australia
	– AbililtyOne Program in the United States
Selling socially conscious products or services	Spectrum Youth and Family Services in Burlington, Vermont, USA
	I AM Scarsdale in Scarsdale, New York, USA
	Adore Boutique in Grand Rapids, Michigan, USA
	The GFB in Grand Rapids, Michigan, USA
Social marketing	Ben and Jerry's Ice Cream in Burlington, Vermont, USA
	Peace and Justice Center in Burlington, Vermont, USA
	KSV in New York, New York, USA
Systemic change	Re-Nuble in New York, USA
	Brewery Vivant in Grand Rapids, Michigan, USA
	Social Enterprise Greenhouse in Rhode Island, USA
	Sheffield Social Enterprise Network in Sheffield, England
	Center for Social Innovation in New York, New York, USA
	Camelback Ventures in New Orleans, Louisiana, USA
	Social Enterprise Scotland in Scotland

(Continued)

Social Impact Models	*Examples*
Social movement	Cancer Research Center UK (various locations)
	Peace and Justice Center in Burlington, Vermont, USA
Social financial services or products	Grameen Bank in Dhaka, Bangladesh
	Plum Valley Investments in New York, NY
	Nova Credit in New York, NY
	Social Enterprise Exchange in Sheffield, England

It is also important to note that social enterprises operate on a spectrum. Some are wholeheartedly and completely devoted to their social mission. Others have a social mission that guides their work, but operate with a very commercial mindset daily. To learn more about social impact models, explore Weaver's Social Enterprise Directory. Thus far, we have identified over 1,000 social enterprises across the United States. When I developed the directory, I was on my own mission to identify a social impact model that would help me address issues like poverty, crime, and poor life outcomes in the Bronx, New York, where I was born and raised. This mission ultimately led me to conducting the first large-scale study (my dissertation) of the social, economic, and legal activities of social enterprises in the United States. I then realized that one of the best gifts I could give my community and other communities around the world is the gift of educating people on how they can do social good, while doing economically well. This chapter focused on doing social good. In Chapters 6 and 7, we explore how to do economically well.

Resources

B Lab (https://bcorporation.net/)
B Lab is a nonprofit organization that awards B Corp certification to for-profit businesses that have a social mission. While based in Pennsylvania, its members are businesses all over the world. B Lab has been a driving force behind the development and advancement of the Benefit Corporation legal business entity.

SE Ontario (https://seontario.org/)
SE Ontario is a leading network of social enterprises in the Ontario region of Canada. It offers a social enterprise directory with hundreds of profiles and partners with government to provide various informational, marketing, and financial supports for its social enterprise sector.

Social Enterprise Alliance (https://socialenterprise.us/)
The Social Enterprise Alliance is a leading membership organization for work on social enterprises in the United States. It has various member chapters

across the nation and provides workshops, webinars, and networking events on social enterprise.

Social Enterprise Scotland (https://socialenterprise.scot/)
Social Enterprise Scotland refers to themselves as "The Voice of Social Enterprises in Scotland." The membership network offers a weekly newsletter, membership events, and activities and provides a social enterprise directory. They also offer consulting services for social enterprises and in general strive to strengthen the Scottish social enterprise sector.

Social Enterprise UK (https://www.socialenterprise.org.uk/)
Social Enterprise UK is the leading network of social enterprises in the United Kingdom. They partner with government and run campaigns related to advancing the social enterprise ecosystem in the United Kingdom and beyond.

Weaver's Social Enterprise Directory (http://socialenterprisedirectory.com/)
Weaver's Social Enterprise Directory is a national, online directory that features information about the geographic location, social activities, goods and services, and legal characteristics of social enterprises throughout the United States. The directory features information on over 1,000 social enterprises in the nation.

6 Startup Financing

My main inspiration for writing this book is to answer the question: If we teach good people how to make money, lots of money, will they in turn do more good with it? As a woman who was born and raised in an impoverished community in the Bronx, New York, I have met many people with hearts of gold. They go above and beyond to help others in need, but after a while they fall short because they lack the resources, mindset, education, skills, and network needed to sustain their efforts. As a result, they get drained, exhausted, become even more impoverished, and then resentful because they would give, give, and give and at some point they realize that they weren't giving enough to themselves.

The truth is, if people genuinely want to address pressing social and environmental issues, they will likely need a diversity of startup financing and revenue streams to do so. They will also eventually need a strong network and the knowledge to constantly adapt to the ever-changing entrepreneurial landscape and world. This chapter focuses on all of these factors. It explores various funding opportunities and strategies available for social enterprises. It also examines challenges that social entrepreneurs may face acquiring certain kinds of financing and how to overcome them. Given the flexible legal structure of social enterprises, this chapter aims to guide readers through the financial landscape that is available to social entrepreneurs and organizational leaders in general, regardless of their legal form.

This chapter focuses on the following three questions regarding different areas of funding: (1) what types of funding opportunities exist for social ventures? (2) What kinds of resources or capitals are available that may help social entrepreneurs obtain funding or resources, or save on expenses? And (3) What are some common bootstrapping techniques that social entrepreneurs may use to save on expenses?

The Importance of Startup Financing

Startup financing or funding is the amount of financial investment made into a social enterprise or other organization with the purpose of helping to launch or advance its development. Sometimes it is provided to help launch

DOI: 10.4324/9781003226963-7

an organization overall, but it is often an investment in an organizations' research and development. Seed-stage financing is early financial awards or investment into an organization for proof of concept, which is simply proving that their idea is both feasible and marketable. Early stage financing, however, is financing for companies that have a team in place and a proven concept, but need financing to grow.

Startup financing can be a critical factor in the overall success of an organization. There are a variety of types of funding and I predict that, as the field of social enterprise grows, innovative types of funding will be invented. While the financial sources for starting a social enterprise are diverse, many social entrepreneurs use their personal savings, money from family and/or friends, or obtain a personal loan to start their business. These funding sources are particularly important in the very early stages of a venture. However, as the organization grows from an idea to prototype to offering minimum viable products for sale, the type of startup financing a social enterprise acquires may differ by legal form and may be traditional or grassroots in style.

Table 6.1 shows the startup funding sources from my study of 115 social enterprises in the United States. As Table 6.1 shows, startup investment can be anywhere from zero dollars to the millions. The amount depends on the types of venture and what is needed to launch it, the entrepreneur, and access to resources. In my study, for-profit social enterprises were more likely to acquire larger amounts of startup financing. In regard to the funding source, Figure 6.1 shows a variety of traditional funding sources. As mentioned, most social entrepreneurs fund their organizations with their personal funds in early stages. However, a variety of funding sources exist. Most social entrepreneurs are simply unaware of them so let's explore some options.

Before we discuss funding sources, it's important to note that types of funding sources available for social enterprises often differ by their legal structure (Table 6.2). Social enterprise financing can, at times, be different than financing other businesses or organizations. They are hybrid organizations, which is a concept most people simply don't understand. In fact, many

Table 6.1 Startup Investment

	N	Min	Max	Mean	SD
Startup investment	66	0	3,500,000	176,468	551,508
Startup Investment by Legal Form					
All for-profit	61	0	3,500,000	188,204	572,315
Traditional for-profit	27	0	2,500,000	169,851	485,644
Hybrid law	27	0	3,500,000	245,351	714,027
Nonprofit	5	500	100,000	33,280	41,497

Note: The numbers for minimum, maximum, mean, and standard deviation represent dollars.
Source: Weaver, R. L. (2017). *Social enterprise and the capability approach: Examining the quest to humanize business* (Doctoral dissertation, Rutgers University-Camden Graduate School).

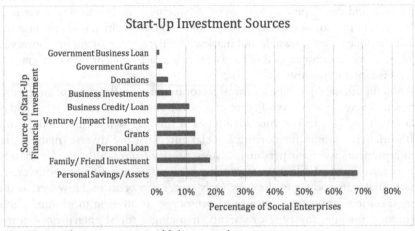

Note: Respondents may report multiple start-up investment sources.

Figure 6.1 Startup Investment Sources.
Source: Weaver, R. L. (2017). *Social enterprise and the capability approach: Examining the quest to humanize business* (Doctoral dissertation, Rutgers University-Camden Graduate School).

Table 6.2 Unique Challenges and Opportunities of For-Profit and Nonprofit Social Enterprises

FPOs	NPOs
For-profit businesses aim to be self-sufficient and have no limits to revenue generation and sources.	Attract volunteers, tax-deductible individual donations, and grants (private, public, and foundation).
As such, they attract investors who want a return on their investment.	Must comply with the non-distribution constraint.
No limits to revenue generation and sources.	Tax-exemption status.

people believe that having a social mission is antithetical to business. Others may even think social enterprise is a scam or tool for an organization's publicity. However, social enterprises are real organizations that prioritize social, economic, and sometimes environmental goals – the People, Planet, Profit approach to entrepreneurship.

Sometimes social enterprises can be for-profit businesses with a social mission or a foundation/social program, a nonprofit organization with for-profit commercial ventures, or a combination of both. As such, the financing options available to social enterprises based on their organizational structure often relate to their goals, as well as the goals of potential investors.

Nonprofit social enterprises have the ability to attract volunteers, tax-deductible individual donations, and grants (private, public, and foundation). These can help with startup costs because social entrepreneurs, for example, could host an informational fundraising event about the good they're trying to do in a community in order to inspire donations. They may also use volunteers for the event to keep costs low. As tax-exempt organizations, they may obtain free bank accounts and exemption from tax on business purchases that ultimately reduce startup expenses. However, the challenge that nonprofit social enterprises face is that they must comply with the non-distribution constraint policy that requires them to distribute all surplus revenue back into the organization as opposed to giving it to directors, shareholders, or investors like in a for-profit business. Another challenge that nonprofit organizations face is the unrelated-business income tax, which fines them if they engage in commercial activities that are unrelated to their social mission.

For-profit businesses aim to be self-sufficient and have no limits to revenue generation and sources. As such, they attract investors who want a return on their investment. Investors, however, are often more concerned with a financial return on profits. Social returns, through the social value created when social enterprises address issues like poverty, unemployment, hunger, or environmental issues, are not easily quantifiable. Thus, while a for-profit structure has the potential for limitless revenue generation, specific legal and/or cultural factors within an organization are needed to ensure a for-profit social enterprise fulfills its social goals.

Types of Startup Financing

Traditional Financing

In this section, traditional funding opportunities such as grants, social impact bonds, venture capitalists, angel investors, and impact investors are discussed. These are more established and well-known funding sources as opposed to the innovative sources that will follow this section.

Grants. A grant is money awarded to an organization, often to fund a specific project or program, that does not have to be returned to the organization. Grants may come from government, philanthropic foundations, community-based organizations, or corporations. Grants may be awarded to a parent organization or directly to a social enterprise. This occurs because social enterprises may be hybrid organizations that have both for-profit and nonprofit entities that ultimately work toward one mission (e.g. Newman's Own and Newman's Own Foundation). For example, social enterprises may operate as a nonprofit organization with a for-profit business "subsidiary" through which they receive grants as a nonprofit parent organization and generate income through their for-profit legal entity. Grants are usually restricted to non-profit organizations.

Program-related investments. Program-related investments (PRIs) are similar to grants in that they aim to fund a social program, but the investor aims to receive a small return on the investment. These investments may be made to parent organizations or directly to a social enterprise. The majority of profits from L3Cs must be reinvested into the business through what is called program-related investments. PRIs ensure L3Cs maintain both a social and an economic bottom-line, as commercial activities must be relevant to its social mission.

Angel investor. Investors who utilize their own money to invest in start-ups, usually young startups, that are founded by people who are usually not friends or family.

Venture capital (also called venture philanthropy funding). A form of grant funding accompanied by high levels of engagement from the funder referred to as a venture capitalist. A *venture capitalist* is a professional investor who invests in early stage businesses and businesses that show great potential. Their goal is to invest in the long-term growth of a company.

Line of credit. A preset amount of money that is a loan to an organization from a financial institution such as a bank or credit union. A number of financial organizations have been developed throughout the world to provide lines of credit specifically for social enterprise.

Social impact bonds. A contract with an organization such as a bank or public institution that strives to "pay-for-success" by investing in successful social service programs and projects of a social enterprise. The goal of the investor, usually called an impact investor, is to amplify their success.

Impact investors. Investors who invest in organizations with the goal of achieving social and/or environmental outcomes in addition to a financial return to their investment. In traditional entrepreneurship, investors are usually focused on financial returns only.

When seeking traditional financing, it is important to understand how investors think. Investors are often looking for businesses that are "bankable," meaning they seem financially healthy and they have "proven" their worth in the market. Most investors are looking for a return on investment (ROI), which means if they invest a particular amount of money into a business, they seek to make a profit on it. They want to ensure that a business will not just vanish overnight after their investment. In other words, they take calculated risks when investing in a business. Terms like bankable and proven often refer to businesses that have at least generated over $1 million in gross annual revenue. However, the beauty of entrepreneurship is that the entrepreneurs define their own success. Some social entrepreneurs may make much less annually, but help a great number of people. Thus, it is important not to be discouraged by someone else's definition of success.

In addition, like all people, investors have different desires and goals. Some are interested in providing patient capital that enables a new business to develop and experiment with products and services. **Patient capital** refers to capital invested into the business that is not expected to make a quick profit. It is understood by the investor that their investment will take time to bear fruit. All in all, there are a variety of different traditional funding opportunities for social enterprises. However, many social entrepreneurs find success using the grassroots options in the following section.

Grassroots Financing

Grassroots-style fundraising is financing that is used in particular communities or by particular groups. They are innovative and context-specific. Grassroots financing includes revenue generated from fundraisers, crowdfunding, giving circles, funding from microfinance institutions, and innovative funding opportunities that intermittently arise in the field.

Fundraisers. A fundraiser is an event or campaign that aims to raise money for a social cause, program, or a nonprofit organization. There is much variation in types of fundraisers. For example, bake sales are a fundraiser. Info sessions that teach friends and family about a particular issue and ask for donations are another example of a fundraiser. Large-scale fundraisers like *Giving Tuesday* that encourage people and organizations to donate to charity are an example of a global fundraising campaign. Just like they vary in terms of size, fundraisers vary in terms of their impact. Some raise small amounts of money and some raise millions.

Crowdfunding. Crowdfunding involves raising money, usually small amounts, from a large group of people usually via the internet. The money raised may be from people an entrepreneur knows, but given the reach of the internet, the money raised is often from a variety of sources. Crowdfunding enables social entrepreneurs to access immediate funds donated to their organization, which is particularly helpful during times of challenge or even crisis (e.g. COVID-19 pandemic).

Collective Giving Circles. Collective giving circles are groups of people who collectively donate money to a cause or organization that they have a mutual interest in. These groups may be informal groups or even groups that move on to form established nonprofit organizations around a social cause. Giving circles exist throughout the world. For example, one of my social entrepreneurship classes has worked with a giving circle called Impact100 Westchester. Impact100 Westchester (one branch of the national Impact100 brand) is a female-only membership group that requires women to pay a membership fee of $1,100 annually to their organization. The membership fees are pooled together to fund local community and economic development projects that have a social cause. One thousand dollars from each member is used toward the fund and $100 from each member is used to cover Impact100 Westchester's operating costs. They have awarded over $2.4 million to projects throughout Westchester, New York, since 2014.

Cultural Savings Clubs or Associations. Similar to a collective giving circle, savings circles involve groups of people coming together to save money for, usually, large purchases in their lives. For example, Rotating Savings and Credit Associations (ROSCAs) are popular among people throughout the African Diaspora. Depending on the country of origin, ROSCAs may be called susu, the partner system, arisan, juntas, tandas, and there are many more terms. Personally, I have witnessed the power of a ROSCA called the Jamaican Partner System where groups of Jamaican women pool their

money together to make large purchases. My mother saved through the partner system for years to buy her first home in the United States. Many examples of such systems are explored in a short movie called "The Banker
Ladies" by Dr. Caroline Hossein of York University. The movie, available on
YouTube, showcases grassroots savings strategies used by black, immigrant
women in Toronto, Canada.

Microfinance organizations. Microfinance organizations are types of financial institutions that target people and small businesses that lack access
to conventional banking and financial institutions. Grameen Bank, for example, is a community development bank that was started by Mohammed
Yunus in Bangladesh. It is famous for offering low-interest loans to impoverished people without requiring collateral. Such organizations can be a great
way to start a business since they are low risk and have a social mission that
focuses on helping the lender. In addition, many microfinance institutions
target the development of marginalized groups like black people (of all na-
tionalities) and women (e.g. Maggie Lena Walker and the Independent Order
of St. Luke in the United States).

Unique and Sporadic Funding Opportunities. While the social enterprise
sector has been around for about 50 years, it is still "new" to the general
public. In addition, the field is growing and thus new and unique opportunities for funding often pop up. Fellowship and grant programs run by small
organizations or local government offices may be available in some communities. For example, The New Jersey Office of Faith-Based Institutions offers
a Social Enterprise Grant program that finances new social enterprise projects being created by nonprofit organizations. Similarly, social venture pitch
competitions are available in communities throughout the world.

Bootstrapping and Bricolage

While having funding to start your business is important, reducing expenses
is also essential to launching, managing cash flow, and scaling any organization. Thus, I could not write a chapter on startup financing without mention-
ing bootstrapping, which is the process of starting a business or organization
with little to no funding. In a way, bootstrapping is like becoming a "jack
of all trades" for your business in the startup phase. In the startup phase,
founders may have to do everything from managing their own budgets, marketing, product development and design, and more. This may be a rewarding
experience because entrepreneurs gain a variety of skills in the process, along
with the confidence that comes with skill development. Figure 6.2 outlines
some common ways to bootstrap and the following paragraphs help explain
the importance and value of each strategy.

Working From Home. Working from home as opposed to in an office
can significantly reduce startup costs and can work for a variety of different
business types. Naturally, organizations that revolve around activities such as
writing, coaching, online selling, and marketing are the kinds of work that

Figure 6.2 Ways to Bootstrap.

may be done from anywhere in the world. However, other types of businesses that may be run from home include daycare centers, bars, dance clubs, a mini cafe, and any product that can be made at home. Lisa Price, the founder of the natural hair product line Carol's Daughter started mixing, labeling, and selling recipes for hair products from her kitchen. While it is exciting and can even feel "more real" to launch a business by renting or purchasing a property or space for your business, delaying doing so often helps entrepreneurs test the market before making such a costly investment.

Purchasing property. Purchasing a property, if you have the financial capital to do so, can be a useful long-term business strategy. Owning property that is paid off can help a business stay afloat during times of economic prosperity and economic uncertainty. For example, a local entrepreneur in New

Rochelle, New York, runs a restaurant in a building that he owns. When the coronavirus pandemic shocked the world and halted much economic activity, his restaurant was able to survive because he owned the property and thus had no mortgage payment. In addition, the property had several apartment rentals above the restaurant that kept income coming in despite declining restaurant sales.

Coworking. Coworking is defined as shared office spaces among workers that enables them to save money on overall business costs. Business costs may include equipment, utilities, food, receptionists, and custodial services. Entrepreneurial coworking spaces, like the one offered by WeWork, have become popular in the last decade. One reason, a part from reduced operational costs, is that many entrepreneurs have a chance to share knowledge, exchange ideas, meet investors, and may form facilitated collaborations simply from working in the same space.

Buying used equipment and furniture. Entrepreneurs who need a physical space for their office or business can purchase used equipment and furniture to reduce expenses instead of purchasing new furniture. I have visited beautifully decorated businesses where almost everything in their rooms were bought secondhand. The trick is, of course, to find quality used equipment and furniture. There are special stores for this and sometimes other businesses may simply be redecorating or closing and will sell their furniture at a low cost or for free.

Forgoing/decreasing salary. Forgoing or taking a small salary in order to re-invest that money into a business is a good technique for launching or growing a business. Some entrepreneurs may even choose to keep their salary, but reinvest all profits back into their company to watch it grow.

Basic legal and accounting information. One piece of advice that I give all new entrepreneurs is to understand the basic legal and accounting information needed to run a business. I personally feel that it is unwise to communicate with a lawyer or accountant without understanding the basics of what they do and what skills you need them for. In fact, I suggest reading multiple books, watching informational videos, and possibly even attending business accounting workshops and business law conferences to stay up to date on legal information. This enables entrepreneurs to have educated and more confident discussions with the people you are hiring to control an incredibly important part of your organization.

Frugal Travel. Entrepreneurs often travel for conferences, meetings, manufacturing, or research. While it is tempting to fly business class and stay in a fancy hotel, in the very beginning stages of entrepreneurship, it can be valuable to invest excess funds toward products and services that are generating revenue or have the potential to. When the organization starts to flourish, then you can upgrade or even splurge. However, when bootstrapping, keep it simple, but still comfortable.

Hire an Intern. Paid and unpaid interns can push projects forward and can even provide an energy boost to entrepreneurs.

Hire Temporary Workers and Outsourcing Tasks. Temporary workers are useful for outsourcing operational tasks like proofreading, editing, painting, hanging art, and more. This enables entrepreneurs to focus their energy doing work that they are specialized in while still completing administrative work.

Networking. We all know that networking is very important in business. However, when thinking about networking from a community development lens, it is essential to build relationships with people who have power and resources. Some great ways to network with such people are to attend workshops, meetings, and conferences that convene people who all want to achieve great things. In addition, look around you and consider having a weekly meeting with people at work or in your community (e.g. president of the local neighborhood group) in order to build relationships. Networking is tricky because people often approach it from a perspective of acquiring or taking something from others. However, a strategic entrepreneur would find ways to be of value to powerful or resourceful people. After all, the best relationships are reciprocal ones. No one wants to give, give, and give and end up feeling used. Thus, ensure to nurture and be of benefit to your network.

Offer Customer Discounts. In the early stages, many businesses offer products or services at lower prices or discounts that enable prospective customers to try and assess a product or service. If they like the product or service, they will likely return for more and spread the word to their friends and family.

Negotiate Payment Terms. Negotiate. Negotiate. Negotiate. I am a big fan of negotiation because many people could get a better deal on something if they simply ask for one. However, I recommend reading a book on negotiating to learn what it truly means and strategies to make it work for you.

Keep Your Day Job. I will say that this suggestion is debatable. Previous research on entrepreneurial training programs have shown they benefit the unemployed the most because they deeply desire employment and thus the training enables them to create their own. However, if you do have a job or career, it may help fund your venture, but it could also cause burnout. Some entrepreneurs are able to work full-time while managing a business on the side, but that is not sustainable or healthy for most people. In order for you to be present and available to run a social enterprise, you need to be mentally and physically healthy so make it a priority.

In addition to bootstrapping, the term bricolage, in the field of entrepreneurship, refers to the process of using resources that are available as opposed to purchasing and searching for new or additional resources. While the definition is similar to bootstrapping, it emphasizes the importance of examining one's environment to identify ways to save money, make money, and to acquire resources. For example, college students who aspire to be entrepreneurs may, at first, seek out resources on their own. However, if they are keeping bricolage in mind, they would utilize campus resources like an entrepreneurship center to attend educational workshops and strengthen their network, their college or university alumni network to find mentors, partners, and possible investors, the campus library to use books and computers for free, campus business competitions to acquire startup funding, and more.

In addition, the term **strategic frugality** refers to the process of only or mainly spending money on revenue-generating activities. The idea is that if selling a particular product or service is working for an organization, then they should continuously invest in that product or service by increasing production or application of it. Strategic frugality is particularly important during times of crisis and economic uncertainty for a social enterprise. Instead of operating business as usual, social enterprises should limit or halt spending on non-revenue-generating business expenses. One example of strategic frugality is continuously reinvesting profits into your organization in an effort to grow. This strategy is particularly important when an entrepreneur desires growth, but is unsuccessful at acquiring external financing such as loans, grants, and investments. Research has shown that this is likely to happen to women and people of color.

Conclusion

Once again, one of the main reasons I wrote this book is to answer the question "If we teach good people how to make money, lots of money, will they in turn do more good with it?" This chapter is critical to answering this question because the information within it aims to put aspiring social entrepreneurs on a path toward acquiring the funding needed to launch and grow their business. It describes traditional and grassroots financing opportunities for social entrepreneurs. In addition, it outlines 13 different bootstrapping techniques for starting a venture. As discussed, there are a variety of financing options and examples of successful social enterprises that have utilized them. Remember, entrepreneurship, whether commercial or social, is in large part about creating your own opportunities. There is no right way to be a social entrepreneur and thus no right path to take. I recommend exploring the options available in your local and regional community in addition to the opportunities in the field at large.

Resources

Ashoka (https://www.ashoka.org/en-us/focus/social-entrepreneurship)
Since 1980, Ashoka has been a leading organization in the development of social entrepreneurship as a field. It is a community of social entrepreneurs and proponents of the field that provide educational opportunities and funding competitions related to supporting social entrepreneurs.

Skoll World Forum (http://skoll.org/skoll-world-forum/)
The Skoll World Forum is an international conference that celebrates social entrepreneurs throughout the world. It is an event hosted by the Skoll

Foundation, which financially and intellectually invests in social entrepreneurs focused on society's most pressing problems.

Fowler Global Social Innovation Challenge (https://www.sandiego. edu/cpc/gsic/)

This social venture pitch competition awards up to $50,000 in funding and additional resources to students to develop a social venture that addresses a social and environmental problem.

7 Revenue Models

I've spent the last seven years studying over 1,000 social enterprises in order to examine their social and economic activities. At first, my goal was to use the information to create a social enterprise myself using best practices among the social enterprises that I studied. However, I firmly believe that every person is born with a gift that needs to be identified, nurtured, and strengthened over time (more on this in the Conclusion of this book). Many people do not take the time needed to reflect on their life's experiences, listen to what others like, emulate and seek in them, and expose themselves to diverse situations that challenge them. Having done these things myself, I have been able to effectively discover my gifts and to strategically utilize them to improve the lives of others as well as my own.

My gift is being able to observe, consume, and communicate a great deal of difficult information and to express it back to other people in a way that is easily digestible and inspirational. This quality is what makes me a great social scientist and an educator. Like most people's gift, it is incredibly easy for me to do and I find it fun. After teaching over 1,000 students in my time as a professor, I believe that it is the *ease* of our gifts that make us overlook them. After embracing my own gift, I realized that it would be much more beneficial to the world if I use my gift to inspire, educate, and equip aspiring social entrepreneurs with the tools they need to create successful social enterprises. As such, this chapter explores answers to the questions:

- Can your idea generate revenue?
- What can you sell in order to generate revenue?
- How many units (products or services) do you need to sell in order to be profitable?
- What happens if it takes a while (e.g. five years) to make a profit?
- How long do you see yourself running this business?
- How much are customers willing to pay for your products and services?
- How many customers do you need in order to break even?
- How much revenue can you generate through sales?
- If there are multiple streams of revenue, how much will you need from each to break even or to make a profit?

DOI: 10.4324/9781003226963-8

The questions above are commonly asked by entrepreneurs, regardless of field or industry. This chapter answers them by outlining various revenue models and income stream opportunities for social enterprises. There are a myriad of ways that social enterprises and institutions in general can generate revenue needed to support their operations and growth.

Revenue

Revenue is the income gained from selling goods and services. **Gross revenue** is the total income generated through sales without deducting expenses from any source. Expenses may include salary, loans, rent, taxes, and other operational costs of running a business. Gross revenue is important for understanding the overall valuation of a business because it assesses how much the business has the potential of making, especially if expenses were reduced. **Net revenue (also referred to as net profit)** is the total income generated minus expenses, returned products or refunded services, and discounts. Net revenue reveals the true profit a business makes. **Profit** may be defined as the financial gain from selling a product or service that is made after deducting expenses. Profits may include the financial gain made from an investment. It is the difference between the amount of money made from that which was invested.

What Are Revenue Sources?

Social enterprises generate revenue from a variety of sources, but the main sources differ by region and organizational/legal structure. In my study of 115 social enterprises across the United States, the average social enterprise generates $1,263,115 in gross annual revenue. On average, these respondents are around 10 years old, have around ten employees, and have a mean of $40,000 in startup investment. This finding is important because many people assume that social organizations do not generate substantial revenues. However, any socially conscious organization that aims to create substantial change will have to. My research found that as social enterprises age, they generate higher revenues. While this may seem obvious, many new entrepreneurs are discouraged by lack of immediate financial success. Yet, businesses take time to grow, evolve, and for people to learn about and trust them. In regard to legal structure, the nonprofit social enterprises had higher revenues, but they were usually older and had more employees than for-profit social enterprises.

In regard to revenue sources, my research found that 97% of social enterprises generate revenue from sales, 24% from grants, and 11% from impact investments. Eighty percent of social enterprises receive at least 50% of their revenue from sales; however, studies suggest that social enterprises in the United States strongly utilize commercial revenue to meet their economic bottom-line. On the contrary, social enterprises in various other nations sometimes have a higher reliance on funding from government and other third-party sources.

Revenue and Income Sources

Sales of Consumer Goods – **Consumer goods** are the most common type of good that social enterprises sell. They consist of products that clients or consumers purchase for consumption. From home furnishing to medical supplies, social enterprises sell a diversity of consumer goods. Some consumer goods are created by social enterprise beneficiaries. For example, some social enterprises that work with refugees aim to increase their economic self-sufficiency by enabling them to generate revenue by selling traditional arts and crafts that they create. Social enterprises generally sell consumer goods on a case-by-case basis, as opposed to contract services (below).

Sale of services or fee for service. This payment model involves customers paying fees for one or more services as opposed to product(s). Selling service-based products differs from selling physical products. With physical products, people can feel, see, and experience their immediate gratification. With services, customers need to use their imagination in order to assess whether or not a service is worthy of purchasing.

Contracts or contract services – Contract services are services that social enterprises offer under a formal, legally binding contract. Contract services sometimes involve subscriptions for products, but can also include services that consumers receive for a specific time-period. Some examples of contract services are: catering, home/business meal-service delivery, custodial service, health insurance plans, credit card processing, or website hosting.

Education and training services are those that develop the knowledge or skills of consumers. Some services involve skill development for general or self-employment opportunities (e.g. knitting classes). Other services aim to increase knowledge through materials and means of communication such as books, TV shows, or informational workshops (e.g. sexual assault prevention classes).

Grants are non-repayable funds that are disbursed to an awardee, usually a nonprofit organization, educational institution, or an individual. Grants are usually awarded by a foundation, corporation, or government organization.

Donations are something, usually money, that is given to a charity, nonprofit organization, or social cause. While most donations are monetary, *in-kind donations* are gifts that are non-monetary but valuable such as resources, goods, services, databases, and land. Donations may be made by anyone, but in the field of social enterprise, they are usually made by individual donors, corporate donors, and board member donors.

Subscriptions are a payment model where customers pay a recurring fee for access to a product or service. The fee is usually processed in advance in order to receive the product.

Membership Fees are regular or recurring fees from a membership organization in order to be a part of a membership community.

Property management or brokering services involve buying, selling, or developing residential or commercial property. Some examples of these services may include land leasing, home sales, architecture and development services, and home rehabilitation services. Property management services, like all social enterprise services, may directly or indirectly relate to their social mission. For example, a direct relation to a social mission may be when a social enterprise buys distressed homes to resell them as an opportunity for affordable housing in a low-income community.

Relationship Between a Good or Service to the Social Mission

Social enterprises have a dual mission in that they pursue social goals and economic goals. However, the missions often, but do not always, overlap. As shown in Figure 7.1, social enterprises may sell goods and services that are simply a financial resource without any relation to their social mission, those that are both a financial resource and that directly relate to the social mission, and goods and services that are a financial resource that finance social mission activities (Table 7.1).

Revenue Concentration vs. Revenue Diversification

When launching an organization, social entrepreneurs may be tempted or inspired to sell a variety of products and services at once. They may even sell different kinds of products or services to different customer segments. In doing so, entrepreneurs are diversifying their revenue streams as opposed to revenue concentration. **Revenue diversification** is when revenue generated by an organization derives from various sources and customer bases. **Revenue concentration** is when a high level or the majority of revenue is generated from one source or customer base.

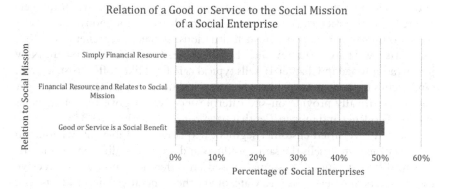

Figure 7.1 Relationship Between a Good or Service to the Social Mission.
Source: Weaver, R. L. (2017). *Social enterprise and the capability approach: Examining the quest to humanize business* (PhD dissertation, Rutgers University-Camden Graduate School, 2017).

Table 7.1 Examples of the Relationship Between a Good or Service to the Social Mission

Organization	Social Mission	Economic Mission
Newman's Own	Donating all profits to various charities and nonprofit organizations through the Newman's Own Foundation. Donations support projects related to veterans, animal welfare, children and families with disabilities, and nutritional well-being.	Selling food products such as beverages, pasta sauces, breathe mints, and salad dressing.
Warby Parker	Donating a pair of glasses to people in developing countries who cannot afford them, which often affects their ability to obtain employment. Also training them to become entrepreneurs who sell glasses.	Generating revenue through selling affordable and stylish glasses.
The Woman's Bean Project	Hiring women to work in their factory, providing them job experience and training, and helping them transition to more advanced career opportunities.	Running a factory that sells beans, jewelry, and canned soups at stores, as well as working with corporations to receive grants.

Whether or not an organization should concentrate on one revenue source or multiple depends on the array (or lack thereof) of products or services they produce. In a study of 200 charities, nonprofits that engage in revenue concentration have higher revenues over time. However, depending on target market and geographic area, revenue diversification may be important for social enterprises to survive and thrive. Some social enterprises operate in markets where target beneficiaries or customers are unable to pay for goods and services or can only pay partial costs. In such situations, social entrepreneurs seek out innovative ways to create revenue. For example, CK Café in Camden, New Jersey (mentioned in Chapter 1), sells typical café food like coffee, pastries, and sandwiches to the general public. However, it shuts down for several hours per day to specifically provide on-site catering services for government agencies and local colleges and universities that have contracts with them. This example illustrates a diversified customer segment (explained in Table 7.2) wherein an organization (often) sells the same products and services at different profitabilities to different types of customers based on differences in how they receive the products and services. CK Café offers the general public products, but offers contracted customers an exclusive experience and physical space.

Nonprofit organizations usually rely on a diverse mix of revenue sources, including (a) income from donations (from private individuals and

Table 7.2 Types of Customer Segments

Customer Segment	Description	Examples
Mass market	A large scale market. The general public.	Electronics industry Department stores
Niche market	A specific, as opposed to general, segment of a market. This market requires specialized offerings.	Companies with niche supplier–buyer partnerships (e.g. Whole Foods Market)
Segmented	Customers with slightly different needs and problems	Retail stores Restaurants Cafes
Diversified	Unrelated customer segments	E-commerce companies (e.g. Amazon)
Multi-sided platforms (multi-sided markets)	Two or more interdependent customer segments	Credit card companies

Source: Osterwalder, A., & Pigneur, Y. (2010). *Business model generation: A handbook for visionaries, game changers, and challengers* (Vol. 1). John Wiley & Sons.

enterprises), (b) income from government through grants, contracts, and services, (c) income from service fees and products sold, and (d) income from investments. In the case of for-profit social enterprises, revenue diversification is less common. Going back to the study of 115 social enterprises in the United States, 80% of social enterprises generate more than 50% of their income from sales.

When considering whether to focus on revenue concentration or diversification, target and available customer segments should be considered. **Customer segments** are different groups of people or organizations that a business aims to reach and serve. The book *Business Model Generation: A Handbook for Visionaries, Game Changers, and Challengers* explains that customer groups are separate segments if: (1) their needs require and justify a distinct offer, (2) they are reached through different distribution channels, (3) they require different types of relationships, (4) they have substantially different profitabilities, and (5) they are willing to pay for different aspects of the offer.

Many people speak of business customers as if they are a general group, but they may indeed be segmented. For example, most customers walk into clothing stores or purchase from their website. Those customers are offered products at a listed price. However, the same clothing store may offer personal shopping services or custom fittings in private rooms that completely change the customer experience. Such customers may be charged higher prices than walk-in customers because of the unique, specialized experience they are being offered.

What Is a Revenue Model?

While **revenue** is the income gained from selling goods and services, a **revenue model** is a model or framework that determines how a business or organization will generate revenue, cover expenses, and make profits. This model helps entrepreneurs to determine what revenue sources to pursue, what value they offer, how to price products and services, and who will pay for their products and services. An entrepreneur's revenue is critical to his or her success.

The model should include the answer to questions such as:

- How much are customers willing to pay for your products and services?
- How many customers do you need in order to break even, which means to cover expenses?
- How much revenue can you generate through sales?
- If there are multiple streams of revenue, how much will you need from each to break even or to make a profit.

Innovative Revenue Generation Sources and Strategies

Buy Social Movement. The buy social movement aims to inspire government, businesses, and the public to purchase from social enterprises as a way of stimulating social good. The main idea behind the movement is to educate people to recognize the social impact they can make through their purchases – their purchasing power! There are two main ways that the buy social movement takes form: (1) The general promotion of "buying social" and (2) the development and/or brokering of targeted partnerships for "social purchasing." In regard to general promotion, countries like Jamaica, the United States, and many more have initiatives that encourage people to purchase from social enterprises. However, these are very small-scale initiatives, usually run by specific organizations, government agencies, or individual social entrepreneurs hoping to start a large movement. Some organizations have even started websites where socially conscious consumers may purchase solely from social entrepreneurs like Toasting Good (USA).

Targeted partnerships for social procurement, on the other hand, are often brokered through a social enterprise support organization that connects social enterprise "suppliers" to social "buyers" in an effort to stimulate social impact. For example, Buy Social Canada is registered as a Community Contribution Company and operates in Vancouver, Canada. They run a social procurement program that aims to educate and promote social enterprises and their impact, certify social enterprises as suppliers of social impact, and attract and engage government, nonprofit organizations, businesses, and universities to become "social purchasing partners." Buy Social Canada is active in community development in the sense that some of its procurement projects focus on creating community benefit agreements, contracts between private organizations and community groups to outline the specific benefits the group will provide to the community.

Another example of the development of targeted partnerships is Social Traders, a not-for-profit organization in Melbourne, Australia, that creates employment opportunities for disadvantaged populations working at social enterprises throughout Australia. Established in 2008, it facilitates social procurement through acquiring government and business "buyers" of social impact and connecting them to social enterprise "suppliers" of social impact. Social Traders joined forces with the Australian Centre for Philanthropy and Nonprofit Studies to conduct a nation-wide study of Australia's social enterprise sector. One outcome of this research was the creation of an online directory called the Australian Social Enterprise Finder, which has since been repurposed to serve as a social procurement membership tool. As of 2020, they have 95 buyer members and 600 certified social enterprise supplier members. They have secured over $105 million in social procurement partnerships.

Social Procurement. As mentioned in Chapter 5, social procurement is the acquisition of a range of assets and services with the aim of intentionally creating social outcomes (both directly and indirectly). The work of Social Traders and Buy Social Canada are examples of social procurement. A number of government bodies around the world are turning to social procurement to advance community development led by social enterprises. This strategy stems from a growing body of research that explores the use of social enterprises as a remedy for longstanding social problems. With the number of social enterprises increasing throughout the world, it is imperative to understand what they do, how they do it, and what supports are needed to facilitate their work.

Community Benefit Agreements (CBAs). An agreement made between an organization and a social enterprise (often through an intermediary organization or even an advocacy group) that establishes the organization's commitment to improving/contributing to the community. CBAs are not just for social enterprises.

Common Financial Challenges for Social Enterprises

Crisis Management, Emergency Funds, and Mechanisms. I could not write this book during the COVID-19 pandemic without including a section that highlights financial challenges related to businesses during uncertain times. At the beginning of the pandemic, I immediately launched a research project on social enterprise resilience in economically uncertain times. One article from this project is entitled "Winter Always Comes: Social Enterprises in Times of Crisis." The idea behind the article is to convey the importance of preparation for difficult times (winter) because winter always comes. Some winters are harsher than others, but they always come eventually, and they are always colder than spring and summer. Social enterprises may account for winter by first acknowledging that it will come, develop a crisis management plan with scenarios on how to handle different challenges that could arise, and dedicate funds for difficulties that arise as well as for innovation (more on that below). In some areas, winter calls for the purchasing of boots, coats, gloves, snowplows, shovels, salt, heaters, and more. Expect this in difficult times and aim to prepare by dedicating some profits to crisis management. Consider it an investment in the long-term social enterprise sustainability … because it is.

Investing in Growth and Innovation. During the COVID-19 pandemic, businesses and organizations of all kinds found themselves constantly needing to rapidly innovate to attend to fast-changing circumstances such as closing their stores and limits on the number of customers allowed inside stores. Some found themselves suddenly thrusted into the world of e-commerce. Others found themselves having to completely innovate their operational spaces by installing plexiglass and purchasing large volumes of masks and hand sanitizers for workers and customers. While businesses that have a budget for growth and innovation are quickly able to adapt, those that do not … likely could not.

With this in mind, it is imperative that new social enterprises, and organizations of all kinds, prepare for growth and innovation before you plan to grow and innovate because the world may force your growth. No one expected a pandemic, that lasted over two years, to occur but it has nonetheless. Future entrepreneurs should set aside some profits for crisis and growth funds to attend to unexpected demands on their businesses.

Know where to invest money. Many social entrepreneurs are interested in acquiring investment capital for scaling their organizations. However, some are unsure of how to best utilize their investment funds. While investment depends on the organization, research has shown that investing in activities that help you generate more revenue are essential to growth. However, seeking counsel from experienced entrepreneurs, going to conferences focused on investing in businesses, and seeking an advisor to gain knowledge about investment readiness would, in and of itself, be a worthwhile investment.

Conclusion

Recall that the mission of this book is to guide aspiring and current social entrepreneurs in the development of sustainable social enterprises. Revenue generation and modeling are essential to that mission. **Revenue** is the income gained from selling goods and services. It is one of the most important factors in operating your business. Without a solid revenue model, social entrepreneurs cannot continuously finance their social programs and activities. While revenue generation may be an intimidating concept to some, I highly recommend social entrepreneurs became comfortable understanding, managing, and striving to advance their financial literacy and strategy. One of the most common reasons organizations, of any kind, fail is poor cash flow management. The truth is, if you want to create an organization that does great work (especially for years to come), it must be sustainable. The social mission of a social enterprise is the heart and soul of the business. However, the economic value created through revenue generation and any way revenue is gained or saved in an organization (e.g. tax incentives, tax exemption, in-kind resources) is of paramount importance to creating social value.

8 Business Planning and Launching

A business plan is like a guide or a roadmap for launching or transforming a venture. In the case of social enterprises, business plans are particularly important for adapting to the unique entrepreneurial environment where social entrepreneurs operate. Unlike traditional for-profit businesses, social enterprises have to consider their social mission, how their work influences beneficiaries, and how much involvement they and other stakeholders should have in the organization. Other factors that need to be considered include exploring the variety of laws that social enterprises may operate under, how to measure social impact, how to attract investment that considers more than just monetary outcomes, and how to convey social enterprise value to people who do not understand or even flat out reject the concept of social entrepreneurship. There is a lot of information to be discussed and explored when it comes to social enterprise business planning.

In addition to serving as a tool for guiding social entrepreneurs in their entrepreneurial journey, business plans may also serve as inspirational documents that keep entrepreneurs motivated and focused on their goals. Business plans (especially the lean business model canvas (LBMC) discussed in this chapter) also serve as a tool for communicating the vision of an organization to others such as investors, banks, government officials, and even new employees. Many social enterprises also work with volunteers who have a tendency to be temporary or seasonal. As such, business plans may be useful for communicating the vision or overall mission of the organization to new people who are continuously cycling through the organization. Overall, business plans are a useful tool for entrepreneurs, employees, executive board members, grant organizations, banks, accelerators, incubators, and investors.

A core goal of this book is to emphasize that social enterprises must be as economically sustainable, innovative, and adaptive as any successful entrepreneurial venture. As such, this chapter explains both the differences and similarities related to business planning for a commercial enterprise and a social enterprise. New business planning tools like the LBMC and the social business model canvas (SBMC) are discussed. This chapter is organized into three parts. The first section outlines major components of a social enterprise business plan. The second section outlines tools for developing a social

DOI: 10.4324/9781003226963-9

enterprise business plan. The final section outlines ecosystem and risk considerations that social entrepreneurs should consider before launching a venture. Examples of traditional and lean business plans, accelerators, and incubators are also provided. Lastly, a general social enterprise checklist is also provided at the end of the chapter that describes important actions that entrepreneurs should take when starting a venture.

Theory of Positive Social Change – The Vision Behind the Business Plan[1]

While you may have heard of a theory of change before, I emphasize that social entrepreneurs should develop *a theory of positive social change*. Positive social change may be defined as transformational processes to advance societal well-being. It is important to recognize that social change may be positive or negative. For example, the acceleration of racially motivated attacks on African Americans and Asians in the United States during the 2020 Presidential election and the COVID-19 pandemic is indeed a form of social change, but it is a negative form of social change. Positive social change occurs when people are benefitted and not hurt. It occurs when the ethics and morals behind activities are sound.

Figure 8.1 shows the process of transforming social problems into opportunities for positive social change. When it comes to developing a theory of positive social change, social enterprise is the medium through which that occurs. The business model, social impact model, revenue model, and legal structure all work together for this *process* to occur and they are all influenced by context. Table 8.1 outlines a basic framework for entrepreneurs to use when developing their theory of positive social change. First, a clear definition of the social problem is needed to develop an adequate solution. Then, a set of assumptions regarding why the problem exists should be outlined.

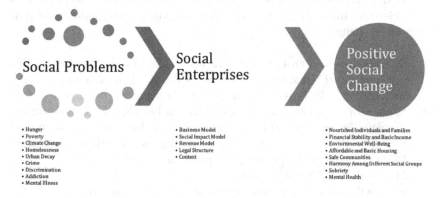

Figure 8.1 Social Enterprise as an Intervention for Social Problems.
Note: The social problems and outcomes in this figure are not exhaustive.

Table 8.1 Basic Theory of Positive Social Change (Nailing the Vision)

Problem	Assumptions	Intervention	Short-Term Positive Social Change Goal	Long-Term Positive Social Change Goal
A diversity of social problems hinder human development and potential.	There are a variety of human and community development strategies, but they are unsustainable and ineffective at eradicating social problems.	Social enterprises are a social intervention, in the form of a business, that aim to advance human development.	Social enterprises foster opportunities to meet diverse human needs through the social services or products that they sell, develop, or support.	Through fostering opportunities, social enterprises seek to reduce or eradicate the human needs of their target beneficiaries, which ultimately results in positive social change.

Next, a social enterprise intervention should be developed to demonstrate *how* the social enterprise aims to solve the problem. The last two columns focus on the short- and long-term goals or outcomes that are expected from a social enterprise intervention.

This simple, but effective framework for outlining a social entrepreneur's theory of positive social change serves as a guiding vision through which social entrepreneurs may move toward throughout their entrepreneurial journey. Such a theory may focus on the local or systemic level. It may also start locally or systemically and evolve to be the opposite over time. Once the theory of positive social change is developed, it is easier to develop a business plan. Here are some questions to consider when developing a theory of positive social change:

1   What is the social problem that you would like to address or solve? Why is it important? What is the root cause of the problem? What factors (e.g. social, economic, historical, contextual) contribute to the problem?
2   What will the mission of your organization be? How will you solve the problem? What other strategies (entrepreneurial or not) have been used to address the same problem? What were the results of those strategies?
3   What does successfully solving the problem look like to you?
4   How will you generate revenue?
5   How will you test your assumptions about solving this problem?
6   Is your theory of change based on research?
7   Are there "leaps of faith" in the theory?

Types of Business Plans

Before we can explore business planning components, we must discuss that there are different kinds of business plans. Traditional business plans are usually between 10 and 20 pages long. As shown in Table 8.2, traditional business plans provide information related to the company description, products and services to be sold, marketing information, operational plans and (if applicable) spatial designs, information on who is managing the organization and other personnel, startup expenses, startup investment, and revenue projections. Traditional business plans aim to be all-inclusive. They provide a good deal of detail on an organization in an effort to communicate that information to various parties and to guide entrepreneurs in their work. It is a long document that is still useful today in some circumstances. Banks and government organizations may seek to have a traditional business plan for loans, contracts, and grants. This section will not explore the traditional business plan sections in detail.

Lean business planning, on the other hand, is a newer, modern form of business planning based on the lean startup methodology (shown in Figure 8.2) by Eric Ries the author of the bestselling book "*The Lean Startup: How Today's Entrepreneurs Use Continuous Innovation to Create Radically Successful Businesses.*" The primary goal of the LBMC is to communicate the most important factors related to a business model on a single page as shown in Figure 8.3.

The components of the LBMC differ from that of a traditional business plan. They are much more concrete, innovative, and targeted in the sense that

Table 8.2 Differences in "Traditional" Social and Commercial Business Plans

Social Enterprise Business Plan Headings	Commercial Business Plan Headings
Cover page	Cover page
Acknowledgments	Contents page
Executive summary	General company description
Background	Products and services
Demonstrating the need for the organization	Marketing plan
Description of the organization	Operational plan
Mission, values, objectives, and activities	Management and organization
Stakeholder analysis	Personal finance statement
Social accounting audit	Startup expenses and capitalization
Environmental impact	Financial plan
Marketing plan	Appendices
Finance	
Work plan and targets	
Summary remarks and conclusions	
Appendices	

Source: Conway, C. (2008). Business planning training for social enterprise. *Social Enterprise Journal, 4*(1), 57–73.

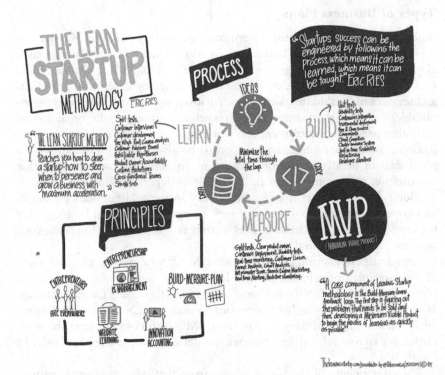

Figure 8.2 The Lean Startup Methodology.
Source: www.theleanstartup.com.

the goal is to rapidly start a business and expect the plan to change over time due to the ever-evolving nature of the 21st century. The LBMC is increasingly utilized by entrepreneurs, investors, incubators, and more. However, the traditional business plan is still valuable for a variety of purposes and industries. In the case of social enterprises, both traditional and LBMCs are utilized and valuable as well. However, the components of each social enterprise business plan differs from the plans for commercial businesses.

As shown in Table 8.1 and Figure 8.4, social enterprise business plans include information related to their social mission such as a stakeholder analysis, social accounting, and a social value proposition. The social business model, in particular, also includes a space for surplus planning. A surplus is the profit an organization makes. When it comes to social enterprises, many (but not all or even most) redistribute their surplus into the company, while commercial enterprises distribute profits to shareholders or directors. Communicating what is done with a surplus is important for transparency in social enterprises, as many funding organizations have requirements of what can be done with social enterprises (more on this in the next section).

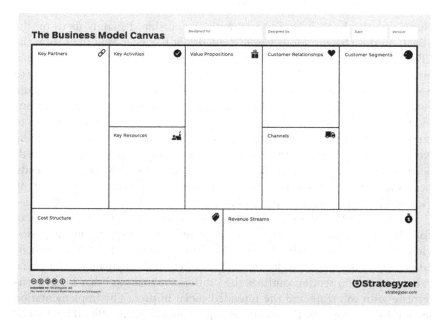

Figure 8.3 Lean Business Model Canvas.
Source: www.theleanstartup.com.

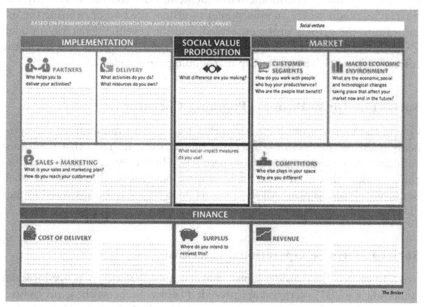

Figure 8.4 The Social Business Model Canvas.
Source: https://socialbusinessdesign.org/what-is-a-social-business-model-canvas/.

Social Business Plan Components

Given that this book is about social entrepreneurship, I mainly focus on the SBMC in this chapter. However, it is important to understand the reason the LBMC emerged as an alternative to the traditional business plan. Traditional business plans tend to be between 10 and 20 pages long, which takes a while to develop, revise, and read. Yet, the world we are living in today is fast-paced and ever-changing. The LBMC enables entrepreneurs to draft, revise, and communicate their business plans quickly. In doing so, it also enables entrepreneurs to innovate expeditiously, which (once again) is important in this ever-changing world. Experienced entrepreneurs understand the importance of constantly educating themselves on the market, consumer behavior, and consumer needs. Learning can be quickly incorporated into the next iteration (as shown in Figure 8.2 from author Eric Ries) of a product or service using the LBMC.

The SBMC offers the same benefits as the LBMC with the added value of considerations related to social value creation, social impact, and surpluses. However, the SBMC is divided into four major components: (1) implementation, (2) social value proposition, (3) market, and (4) finance. The social value proposition section outlines the "difference making" that a social enterprise aims to create and the intended social impact. The implementation section focuses on how the social value proposition being offered by a social enterprise will be delivered (e.g. online, in-person, wholesale), the sales and marketing plan, and the partners who will help deliver the value proposition (in some way). The market section consists of outlining the customer segment, the macroeconomic environment, and the competitors. Lastly, the finance section is where an entrepreneur outlines the cost of running the organization, the surplus/profit generated, and the revenue generation model. Overall, the SBMC is a simplified version of the LBMC that also keeps the core principles of the lean startup methodology in mind.

Social Enterprise Business Planning Checklist

One of the most common questions that I get asked from aspiring entrepreneurs is for me to develop a checklist of activities and tasks that they must consider when business planning so here it is. The following checklist outlines considerations that need to be made or questions that need to be asked when outlining a business plan. All the answers do not need to be answered immediately, as entrepreneurship is a journey filled with lots of iteration (Table 8.3).

Social Enterprise Operational Checklist

In addition to the considerations above, some operational procedures for launching a social enterprise are provided below. Some of these procedures may occur before or after an organization is launched. This checklist does not need to be completed in order (Table 8.4).

Table 8.3 Points and Questions to Consider When Business Planning

Business Planning Stage	Description	Questions/Points to Consider
Vision and people power	• Develop the Vision – Theory of Positive Social Change • Outline the mission statement • Begin cultivating a leadership team and board of advisors (this takes time)	• What would success in this organization look like? What's the vision? • Do the people on the founding team share the social values that are driving the social enterprise?
Revenue modeling	• What is the influence of revenue models on daily operations and long-term sustainability? • How will you acquire, retain, and increase customers over time?	• What are you revenue streams? • What is your burn rate? • What are your fixed and variable costs? • What is your unit cost and how does growth affect the cost? • Sustainability – How much cash do you have on hand to make ends meet? • What are your cash flow projections and income statements for the first one to three years of operations?
Marketing, messaging, and communication	Deciding whether or not to showcase your mission or product first is tricky because social enterprises have been successful at both strategies. Aspiring social entrepreneurs should test the market to assess what is most appropriate. One important thing to consider when designing your social mission is the context where your business is based.	• Will you market the mission or the product first? • Will your social enterprise be in a community where public awareness and support for social organizations is common? For most social entrepreneurs, the answer will be no.
Customer discovery and understanding	When most consumers purchase, they are thinking of their need for the product first. The social impact of purchasing a particular product or shopping at a place that sells socially conscious products overall is usually just a bonus. This does not mean that people do not care about an organization's social mission.	• Who is your target consumer? What are the different customer archetypes? • What are their spending patterns? • How would your product or service bring value to them?

(Continued)

Business Planning Stage	Description	Questions/Points to Consider
	On the contrary, there is a growing consumer base for socially conscious organizations. However, realistically, money leaves people many ways and usually only comes into their life in a few ways. People will thus spend first on their needs.	
Ecosystem and risk considerations	• Community capitals • Competition • Funding opportunities • Strengths, weaknesses, opportunities, and threats in the ecosystem and the organization	• What are the rules of the game (i.e. regulatory, tax, political)? • What is the market need and size of the opportunity? • Competitive landscape: What other approaches to solving the social problem have been tried? • What have been the experiences of other service providers? • What is distinctive about your approach and organization? • How much money flows to your 'issue' annually from all sources and how is it distributed? • How will you capture existing dollars or attract new resources?
Risk management	Risk-taking and risky times are inevitable in business and thus entrepreneurs should strive to prepare for them. While the notion that entrepreneurs are risk-takers is true, to be specific, they are calculated risk-takers. This should not be confused with reckless risk-taking. Calculated risk-taking is about making educated decisions.	• What could go wrong? • Contextually • Strategically • Programmatically • Financially • How will you mitigate these risks?

Note: Some of these considerations were adapted from: Dushin & Dodson. (2015). Developing a social enterprise business plan. Retrieved from: https://www.hbs.edu/newventurecompetition/Documents/SE-TrackDevelopingSEBusinessPlan2015.pdf.

Table 8.4 Startup Operational Checklist

Completion	Task
	Conduct market research
	Write a business plan
	Explore and secure startup financing opportunities
	Choose a business location (e.g. store, online, app, wholesale distribution)
	Choose a business name and search for its availability
	Legally register your business
	Obtain a tax ID
	Obtain a URL for your website
	Apply for licenses and permits
	Open a business bank account
	Decide on a launch plan and get feedback from prospective customers on it
	Launch your organization!
	If appropriate, consider protecting your intellectual property with a patent, trademark, or copyright

Conclusion/Summary

A business plan is a tool that helps social entrepreneurs outline their social mission, along with the infrastructure needed to fulfill it. A good business plan is inspirational, informative, adaptive, and valuable. In order to create the type of sustainable social ventures this book aims to help create, a solid foundation and system for the venture needs to be built. This chapter outlines contemporary and traditional businesses for social and commercial enterprises to deepen knowledge about how to achieve this goal. The SBMC is increasingly utilized by entrepreneurs and utilized by investors, incubators, and more. However, the traditional business plan is still valuable for a variety of purposes as well. Ultimately, the social entrepreneur takes the leadership to decide which plan is best for their organization. However, keep in mind that business plans are "living documents." They should evolve over time as a social entrepreneur learns more about their consumers and how to run their organization as effectively (achieving desired outcomes) and efficiently (achieving desired outcomes at a low cost) as possible.

Note

1 Stephan, U., Patterson, M., Kelly, C., & Mair, J. (2016). Organizations driving positive social change: A review and an integrative framework of change processes. *Journal of Management, 42* (5), 1250–1281.

9 Social Impact Measurement

One of my favorite sayings is "know the value of knowing your value." There are a variety of reasons why social enterprises should measure their social impact, but one of the most important from a business perspective is simply that *when you know your worth, you are better positioned to communicate your worth*. Social enterprises operate in a unique space where they are not traditional for-profit businesses or nonprofit organizations. As such, many people have a difficult time understanding what they are. Some people even think having a social and an economic mission is contrarian. However, the most successful social enterprises that I have witnessed are good at communicating both their unique social and commercial value proposition. However, as mentioned in Chapter 2, measuring social impact is not an easy task.

Less than half of the social enterprises in my study of 115 around the United States report that they do not measure their social impact. There are a variety of reasons for this. Measuring social impact *can be* difficult, time-consuming, and expensive, yet actually doesn't have to be. This chapter takes a dive into the world of social impact measurement. It discusses the importance of measuring social impact, challenges social entrepreneurs face doing so, and outlines various tools for social entrepreneurs to explore. However, it is important to remember that social entrepreneurship is a journey with different stages and milestones. Figuring out how to measure social impact is not essential in the beginning.

What Is Social Impact Measurement?

Social impact measurement involves assessing the social and/or environmental outcomes of social enterprise activities. Social enterprises have a dual (and sometimes a triple bottom-line) structure consisting of the creation of social, environmental, and economic value. While economic value may be easily assessed by calculating the number of sales generated by the organization or the amount of money invested into it, social and environmental value creation can be subjective and difficult to evaluate. However, there are various reasons why a social enterprise should assess their impact, including to better communicate their value proposition, to adequately allocate resources to

DOI: 10.4324/9781003226963-10

social and environmental activities, to demonstrate success or progress, and to provide proof for government and philanthropic funders and investors.

When it comes to value proposition, a value proposition may be defined as the value that a product, service, or organization overall offers its customers and users. However, a **social value proposition** is the value that a product, service, or organization has on its customers, beneficiaries, and other stakeholders. Figure 9.1 outlines social enterprise stakeholders. As organizations with a dual or triple mission, social enterprises are expected to have a positive impact on society. As such, their social value proposition should indicate that in some manner.

Many customers make purchases from social enterprises *because* they are social enterprises. Thus, information about social impact may influence purchasing decisions. For example, I used to serve on the Board of Trustees for the Center for Environmental Transformation (CFET) in Camden, New Jersey, which is one of the poorest cities in the United States.

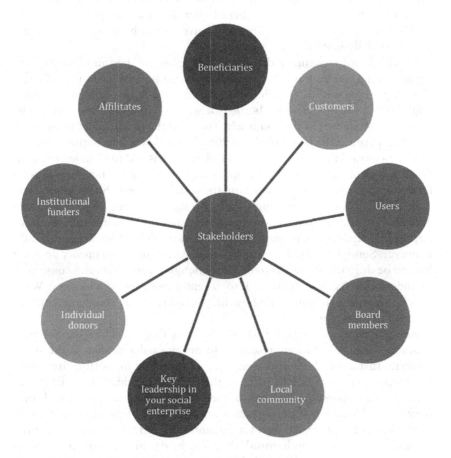

Figure 9.1 Types of Social Enterprise Stakeholders.

When I joined the board in 2017, the high school graduation rate was about 46% and the median household income in the city was approximately $12,000 annually. Naturally, socioeconomic factors like this lead to or are coupled with a host of social problems in the community. One major issue was youth running away from home or going missing. CFET's work focused on educating people about environmental injustice. We had several urban farms and a house that we used for environmental education retreats for church and school groups across the country. The rise in missing children inspired our board members to ask what can we do to combat this issue? Thus, South Camden Farms was born. Under the leadership of Dr. Mark Doorley, Professor and Director of the Ethics Program at Villanova University and President of CFET, South Camden Farms was created to start a youth-run hot sauce company (hot sauce bottles shown in Figure 9.2) using habanero peppers that grow in CFET's urban gardens. The goal of South Camden Farms is to serve as a revenue-generation arm of CFET (a nonprofit organization) that employs youth to sell hot sauce in order to improve their economic self-sufficiency, grant them leadership and entrepreneurial skills, build their confidence, and to ultimately give them a better chance of living a good, socially mobile life.

CFET's board recognized that the reason many children in Camden were going missing was because they needed to escape poverty and the challenges that often come with it (e.g. domestic violence, gang involvement, hunger). Figure 9.2 shows the hot sauce bottle that we developed with the youth. The label states the names of the youth who launched the first product from South Camden Farms, which is called KAPOW! Hot Sauce and outlines that all profits go toward their employment. The hot sauce is sold to Camden residents for $3 and to outsiders for $5. The differentiated pricing has not been an issue for customers because they understand the social mission behind the product.

In regard to social impact measurement, understanding your value as an organization enables you to communicate that value to different social enterprise stakeholders. It is assumed that measuring social impact is difficult. However, South Camden Farms shows that measuring social impact does not have to be difficult. It just has to be clear enough for investors and consumers to understand. As aforementioned, social enterprises are on a journey. What a social enterprise measures and how they measure it may change at different stages of that journey.

Another reason to measure social impact is that it enables social enterprises to adequately allocate resources to operational activities. If the social activities that a social enterprise engages in are found impactful, then more resources could be added to increase the impact. In addition, social entrepreneurs could pursue additional, outside funding opportunities to advance their work. However, if the impact is not measured, they would not know if, when, and how to make such investments. Similarly, if the social activities are not impactful or even harmful, they may be draining the organization of resources that could be allocated elsewhere.

Figure 9.2 KAPOW Hot Sauce.
Source: https://www.app.com/story/entertainment/dining/2018/12/03/new-jersey-food-gifts/2114265002/0.

Another important, and hardly discussed issue, in business is the need to *understand non-quantitative success.* Many entrepreneurs start organizations that are qualitatively successful, but that are not financially growing. In such situations, the organization may have an inappropriate revenue model for the kind of business it's operating or the kind of context it operates within. A **startup** is defined as a new company or project that is seeking to develop a scalable business model. Until an organization has a proven business model that stands on its own, it's essentially a startup. One of the purposes of patient capital (discussed in Chapter 6) is to help an organization find its business model (which is why I'm an advocate for it). It takes time for many entrepreneurs to understand their customers, the market, and what it really takes to build the infrastructure of their business.

Facebook, for example, existed for a few years before it identified a way to consistently generate revenue. However, it had a great deal of qualitative success that inspired investors to take a chance on it. Specifically, people started joining Facebook at alarming rates on different college campuses, then cities, then countries, and ultimately continents. Today, it is one of the most successful businesses to ever exist. However, if Mark Zuckerberg and his co-founders gave up on the idea because it did not generate revenue for a few years, while thousands of people were signing up for it (a qualitative indicator of success), it would not exist today. The qualitative success Facebook had in its early years illustrates its importance in people's lives, as they were logging in daily to post or see their friend's posts. Note that Facebook's users do not pay to use the service. Advertisers are Facebook's main customer segment, but it took time for Facebook to figure that out. The same idea is true for social enterprises. When social enterprises can show qualitative measures of success, then that means they are on the right path, but they must uncover a revenue model or simply a customer segment that is appropriate for the venture.

Last, but not least, another reason to measure social impact is to provide proof for government funders and other investors. The growth of social enterprise as a field has also sparked a movement of funders dedicated to financing such organizations ... if they can show impact. Impact investors, angel investors, government contractors, and social procurement/purchasing brokers are all looking for social enterprises that are making a positive impact on their target beneficiaries to fund and amplify their work.

Ways to Measure Social Impact

There is a major difference between the social activities and the outcomes of those social activities. Simply engaging in social activities does not indicate that they are successful or even accomplishing the goals they aim to fulfill. Not to mention, social entrepreneurs are not always ethical human beings; they may simply be entrepreneurs who see a valuable opportunity in social problems. With all of this in mind, measuring the outcomes of social value creation is important. Various quantitative and qualitative tools exist to measure social impact. Some quantitative tools like Cost-Effectiveness Analysis, Cost–Benefit Analysis, Social Return on Investment by REDF, and B Analytics by B Lab have been developed specifically for measuring social impact. However, the qualitative techniques are mainly techniques that are commonly used in scientific research overall like interviews, focus groups, case studies, and the capability approach.

Quantitative measures aim to translate social outcomes in terms of numbers and the amount of money invested into the social programs. As shown in Table 9.1, many quantitative tools have been developed by social financing firms or organizations to assess the impact of their social investments. They use terms like "monetization" to indicate how social outcomes are being described in monetized terms, giving them a dollar value. Qualitative approaches like interviews, case studies, and focus groups tend to assess deeper impacts and outcomes on the target beneficiaries to assess how their

Table 9.1 Different Social Value Measurement Tools

Measurement Tool	Provider/Developer
Acumen fund BACO ratio	Acumen Fund
AtKisson compass assessment for investors	AtKisson, Inc.
B analytics	B Lab
Balanced scorecard (BS$_C$)	Robert Kaplan and David Norton
Center for high impact philanthropy (CHIP) cost per impact	Center for High Impact Philanthropy
Cost–benefit analysis/benefit–cost analysis	Used and designed differently by different organizations.
Cost-effectiveness analysis	Used and designed differently by different organizations.
Ongoing assessment of social impacts	REDF
Poverty and social impact analysis	The World Bank
Social return assessment	Pacific Community Ventures
Social return on investment	REDF
Theory of change	Used and designed differently by different organizations
William and Flora Hewlett Foundation (Hewlett) Expected Return	William and Flora Hewlett Foundation

Sources
Clark, C., & Rosenzweig, W. (2004). double bottom line project report. *The Rockefeller Foundation*. Retrieved October 1, 2022 from https://escholarship.org/content/qt80n4f1mf/qt80n4f1mf.pdf
Tuan, M. T. (2008). *Measuring and/or estimating social value creation: Insights into eight integrated cost approaches*. Seattle, WA: Bill & Melinda Gates Foundation.

development has changed from the social enterprise intervention. There is much debate among scholars about the ethics of translating social impacts into monetary terms and thus many favor qualitative methods because they provide rich insights on beneficiary outcomes. However, a growing number of scholars suggest that using both quantitative and qualitative tools together are valuable.

A Special Note about the Capability Approach

My research uses a framework called the capability approach to assess the types of social impact that social enterprises create, along with the actual outcomes. I introduced the term social capability to social enterprise research in an effort to emphasize that social enterprise services aim to foster human capabilities. Social capabilities may be easier to measure than social value because they are outlined by the dimensions shown in Figure 9.3 and in the List of Central Social Capabilities on the next page, whereas social value is a broad term with no exact operational definition. On the contrary, definitions for social value are highly debated in the literature, making the term difficult to measure.

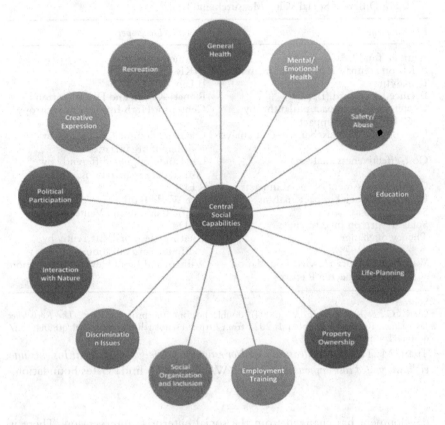

Figure 9.3 Central Social Capabilities.

List of Central Social Capabilities

There are 13 central social capabilities. The list below outlines each based on the theme regarding four core areas of human need that they align with.

Health and Human Security

Social capabilities aim to develop or improve the mental and physical health, life expectancy, and security of human beings.

1 **Health**. Providing opportunities that benefit health (including re-productive), nourishment, and life expectancy.
2 **Mental/emotional health**. Offering opportunities that foster mental health and that advance an individual's ability to connect with other's outside themselves on an emotional level.

3 **Safety or abuse**. Providing opportunities that enable individuals to protect themselves from violent assault or cope after directly or indirectly surviving violent assault.

Social Mobility

Social capabilities related to social mobility aim to advance the socio-economic status of individuals, social groups, or communities. They involve developing the skills and abilities that enable people to increase their human capital, wealth, and life goals.

4 **Education**. Providing services or products that advance educational development. This includes opportunities that foster critical thinking, imagination, and reasoning.
5 **Life-planning/decision making**. Providing opportunities that enable individuals to make plans toward their life goals, as well as to critically reflect on them.
6 **Property ownership**. Providing opportunities that help people obtain and own property, including houses, cars, and other material goods.
7 **Employment training**. Providing opportunities that enable people to prepare and/or obtain employment. This is especially important for those that have difficulty obtaining employment due to lack of skills or systemic discrimination.

Social, Political, and Environmental Engagement

Social capabilities related to social, political, and environmental engagement involve creating opportunities for people to actively participate in society and the social systems that influence their social, political, and environmental well-being.

8 **Social issues and inclusion**. Providing opportunities that enable people to organize around social issues and/or providing spaces of inclusion.
9 **Discrimination issues**. Providing opportunities that enable individuals to deal with issues related to discrimination and/or to mobilize against such issues.
10 **Interaction with nature**. Providing opportunities that foster human interaction with things of nature such as plants, animals, and the overall environment.
11 **Political participation**. Providing opportunities that help people to engage in their political system, informing them of their rights, and/or striving to protecting their rights.

Self-Expression and Social Relationships

These social capabilities focus on fostering human creativity, recreation, and their relationships with other human beings.

12 **Independent/creative expression**. Providing opportunities that enable people to express themselves in a diversity of ways, including through art, religion, and politics.
13 **Recreation or entertainment**. Providing opportunities that foster social interaction and participation in recreational activities that make them laugh or play.

Sources

Weaver, R. L. (2020). Social enterprise and the capability approach: Exploring how social enterprises are humanizing business. *Journal of Nonprofit & Public Sector Marketing*, *32*(5), 427–452.

Weaver, R. L. (2017). *Social enterprise and the capability approach: Examining the quest to humanize business* (Doctoral dissertation, Rutgers University-Camden Graduate School).

I also introduce the term social functionings to indicate the actual impact of social enterprise services on beneficiaries. The term emphasizes that social enterprise services are a means to an end. Specifically, social enterprise services may not result in the achievement of an intended outcome. The term social value indirectly connotes that some value is provided through social enterprise services. The distinction between social capabilities and social functioning indicates a difference between providing a service and achieving a particular impact in a beneficiary's life due to the service provided.

My introduction of the terms social capability and social functioning aims to standardized the way social value is viewed and measured. These definitions relate to how the terms human capabilities and functionings are used in literature on the capability approach by economists Amartya Sen and Martha C. Nussbaum. Human capabilities are the opportunities people have to do things in life that have meaning to them and/or allow them to fully participate in society (e.g. available job opportunities). Functionings are the achievements people make in life regarding their well-being (e.g. securing a job). Functionings are what people *actually do* in life such as voting, working, or going to school.

I used Nussbaum's list as a starting point for my list of central social capabilities. I organize the social capabilities by theme in regard to four core areas of human need: health and human security; social mobility; social, political, and environmental engagement; and self-expression and social relationships.

Health and human security involves creating opportunities that aim to advance or secure the physical and mental health or lifestyles of individuals or communities. Social capabilities in this area are health; mental/emotional health; and safety or abuse. Social mobility involves developing the skills and abilities of individuals, social groups, or communities in an effort to elevate their socioeconomic status over time. These capabilities include education; life-planning/decision making; property ownership; and employment training.

Social, political, and environmental engagement consists of creating opportunities for people to engage in social systems or social causes that relate to their political, social, and environmental well-being. These social capabilities include social issues and inclusion; discrimination issues; political participation, and interaction with animals, plants, or nature. Lastly, self-expression and social relationships involves creating opportunities that foster individual creativity, entertainment, and nurtures the relationships individuals have with others. These social capabilities include independent/creative expression and recreation or entertainment.

While only a few studies apply the capability approach in this manner, more and more researchers and social entrepreneurs are considering it due to the rich insights it provides about beneficiary outcomes. Exploring social value through the capability approach offers a multidimensional account of the social issues that social enterprises aim to alleviate. The workbook and online course that accompany this book include measuring tools and guidance on how to apply the capability approach for social impact measurement, as well as to deepen understanding about the needs of target beneficiaries.

Conclusion

"Knowing the value of knowing your value" is important for communicating your value to a diversity of social enterprise stakeholders. When a social entrepreneur understands their impact, they can discover ways to amplify it, acquire funding for it, and even replicate it across context. However, it is actually not always essential to measure social impact. It is also not an immediate need for the organization during the startup phase. While measures should be put in place for impact assessment, it is much more important to conduct a thorough assessment of the needs of target beneficiaries and consumers. As discussed in Chapter 3, needs assessments allow social enterprises to learn about the social problems in their target community so they can develop empathetic solutions that beneficiary and consumer needs (the main idea behind Design Thinking and empathy mapping). Once a social enterprise has a thorough understanding of their target beneficiaries' needs and have designed an evidence-based solution, they are in a stronger position to assess their impact and to achieve the results they desire.

10 Scaling a Social Enterprise

Warby Parker is a social enterprise that initially launched their business selling prescription glasses online and donating a pair to people from disadvantaged backgrounds for every pair that was purchased. When they started, purchasing prescription glasses online was uncommon, but they launched anyway. Today, Warby Parker now sells glasses online and owns dozens of stores throughout the United States and Canada. While Warby Parker literally scaled their business by creating dozens of stores, there are a variety of ways to scale a social enterprise including by:

- Transforming its organizational structure (e.g. NPO to SE, FPO to hybrid SE)
- Increasing the number of beneficiaries served
- Adding variety to the types of services offered
- Diversifying the types of beneficiaries served
- Multiplying the types of goods and services sold
- Expanding the number of goods and services sold
- Broadening the geographic location where goods and services are sold
- Growing the number of locations where social services are offered
- Deepening the impact of social activities (e.g. policy change)

As you read above, when it comes to scaling a social enterprise, scaling can refer to growing a variety of factors, including customers, operations, employees, beneficiaries, or the organization's geographic reach. This chapter is thus divided into two major sections. The first is growing the organization. The second is growing the social impact and outcomes. In regard to growing the organization, this chapter discusses three different models for scaling a social enterprise with an emphasis on cultivating human resources. The models relate to human capital acquisition, human capital development, and human capital retention. Human capital acquisition involves recruiting staff with essential skills and mindsets. Human capital development consists of training and developing reward and incentive systems that enable them to grow as individuals over time. Human capital retention is the process of striving to keep employees for long periods of time, often through incentive

DOI: 10.4324/9781003226963-11

packages and benefits. In regard to growing the social impact and outcomes, this chapter explores surface-level and deep-level strategies for positive social change. While it is tempting to place one strategy above another, this chapter emphasizes that both have their purpose in the social enterprise movement.

Growing the Organization

When it comes to growing a social enterprise, human capital is one of the most important factors. While previous chapters of this book described human capital, this chapter takes a deeper dive into understanding the role it plays in growing a social venture. Human capital is needed for growing and scaling a social enterprise. It includes talented managers, operational staff, volunteers (if applicable), contractors, and/ or interns. Human capital acquisition involves recruiting staff with essential skills and mindsets.

There are two types of **human capital acquisition**: (1) generic human capital and (2) specialized human capital. Generic human capital involves acquiring people that can perform the basic functions within an organization (e.g. administrative skills, operational capabilities, cashiering). People with these skills, while incredibly valuable, are much easier to find than those with specialized skills. As such, generic skills like accounting, marketing, public relations are applicable to diverse contexts.

Specialized human capital is more context-specific. Specialized human capital consists of acquiring people with a certain kind of expertise, talent, intellectual property, and or a unique access to networks, intellect, or technology. As such, acquiring people with this kind of skillset is more difficult. They may be harder to find and harder to replace than people with generic human capital.

Once a venture recruits the human capital needed to establish or fulfill the work of the organization, **human capital development** begins. Human capital development consists of training and advancing the growth of employees. Some social entrepreneurs may develop formal training procedures and materials in an effort to systematically train incoming employees, as well as those elevating to higher positions. In such situations, training staff may need to be recruited to conduct such training and possibly even to develop the materials and program.

Some social entrepreneurs, however, may want to engage in an informal training process. This may consist of having employees mentored, coached, or shadowed by the social entrepreneur. Considerations about the type of training needed for the organization depend on the entrepreneur's goals. For my organization, Weaver's Social Enterprise Directory, Inc., I developed online training workshops and a training guide for incoming interns and contract workers. It provides such a relief from having to train each person individually and new employees can re-read or replay training materials and recordings, reducing the time I spend fielding questions and ensuring consistent training among new hires.

Table 10.1 Human Capital Retention Challenges and Strategies

Challenges	Strategies
• Turnover affects operations and product/service distribution • Staff that has had specialized training is a lost investment • Environments with little high-skilled workers have a high turnover	• Implement employee contracts for a given duration of time • Recruit staff based on their values in addition to or as opposed to simply their skills • Provide performance-based incentives and rewards

Human capital retention involves retaining existing employees. Employee retention is important for keeping investments made from recruiting, training, and developing the employee during their time with the organization. In addition, every employee who leaves an organization leaves with intellectual capital from that organization. With these considerations in mind, it is important for social enterprises to retain employees. However, there are some challenges that may arise in doing so. Table 10.1 outlines challenges related to human capital retention and some strategies for overcoming them.

Growing the Social Impact and Outcomes

While most, if not all, social enterprise begin as small businesses, many grow to become larger organizations in terms of their social outcomes. Some examples that have already been discussed in this book include Warby Parker, Homeboy Industries, Grameen Bank, Newman's Own, and Seventh Generation. Some of these organizations have a surface-level impact while others have a more deep-level strategy for creating positive social change (PSC).

Surface-level PSC strategies may create change for a large number of beneficiaries, but the change may not be deep or life-altering. Deep-level PSCs, on the other hand, seek to address the diversity of issues their beneficiaries face. Such organizations create numerous social programs for a particular group of beneficiaries (as opposed to increasing the number of their beneficiaries) because doing so provides a more holistic approach to human development. Homeboy Industries, for example, works to rehabilitate gang members back into society. While removing them from gangs and engaging them in the workforce is important, over time the organization created services related to tattoo removal, offering legal counsel, and providing education and etiquette training in order to help them overcome other challenges that impact their reintegration back into society.

It is important to note that, a surface-level PSC such as, for example, running a soup kitchen and feeding 700 people daily may not create massive changes in beneficiary social mobility, but it does literally keep beneficiaries alive. Thus, both surface-level and deep-level PSCs are important for accomplishing different goals.

With all of this in mind, some questions that a social entrepreneur should explore when thinking about growing a social enterprise in terms of its social impact and outcomes are:

- What is the current impact of your social impact model on beneficiaries?
- What supports do your beneficiaries need that you are unaware of?
- If you successfully create positive social outcomes, how do you maximize the value you are trying to create?
- How do you balance the "speed of scaling" with program quality to optimize social value creation?

These questions are important because social enterprise growth is more complex than commercial venture growth (e.g. beneficiaries). Social enterprises face barriers related to both financial sustainability and social impact. Values-based barriers include conflicts over ethical values between stakeholders or having to purposefully reject funders with bad values. Social enterprises have faced moral dilemmas when selling to major retailers (e.g. supermarkets) that sell unethically made products. Some organizations see the risk of compromising their social mission too great to pursue growth. Many social enterprises will even pay more to their suppliers for ethical reasons, resulting in less profit for them.

In regard to business-model growth-based challenges, social enterprises struggle to secure all forms of finance. They struggle to secure growth capital from commercial and social financial sources. Organizations that adopt a commercial legal structure cannot access funds from charities and foundations. Organizations that prohibit financial returns to stakeholders are unattractive to commercial funders like banks and venture capitalists that desire return on investment (ROI) for investors. Many banks also do not understand the concept of social enterprise so they hesitate lending to them. In addition, many social enterprises use their network for human resources. However, this is only as good as the people in one's network. Due to offering lower salaries to employees (particularly in nonprofit social enterprises), because of the need to reinvest money into the social mission, social enterprises have limited pools of human capital and limited rewards for high achievement. Therefore, they often engage in network-based recruitment.

Despite these challenges, there are ways around them. Values-based decision making should be front and center in social entrepreneurship. The decision to prioritize a social mission is what distinguishes social enterprises from other organizational forms. As such, social enterprises should have a focus on developing values-based partnerships in which the commercial and social values are intentionally aligned to guide growth. Care must be taken when recruiting new board members, leaders, and employees to increase their potential for keeping the social enterprise ethical and on track with its theory of positive social change.

In addition, social entrepreneurs should leverage their social mission with investors. Social finance consists of lenders and investors who are committed to finding organizations that drive social change. Some people gain a personal and deep satisfaction from working with a social enterprise. Be clear about social goals with all partners and investors from the beginning and that accomplishing them takes time. Lastly, when social enterprises are anchored in their community, they become a part of its cultural fabric. People become proud to see and experience them. Thus, local anchoring raises awareness, stimulates interest, and prompts purchasing behavior in the local community as well as to wider markets.

Conclusion

Because social enterprises are organizations with dual goals, both their commercial and social activities have the potential for growth. As such, this chapter explores how to grow social enterprise operations by developing both the organization and the social outcomes of the organization. It explores hiring, training, and retaining employees. In addition, it examines considerations to make when seeking to grow social outcomes. Regardless of scaling strategy, social enterprises must remember that sustainability is more important than growth. Having cash reserves and a crisis management program/plan in place is essential to long-term SE growth (which we learned from the COVID-19 pandemic). If a social enterprise has a solid scaling strategy and has proven to be successful, then growth is both good for that enterprise and society. However, it is most important to secure one's organizational foundation before branching off.

11 Social Enterprise Challenges and Success Factors

Henry Ford once said *"Failure is simply the opportunity to begin again, this time more intelligently."* Like all organizations, some social enterprises fail and some succeed. Regardless of the outcome of a social enterprise's journey, there are patterns among those that are successful and those that dissolve. This chapter prepares readers for the common challenges of running a social enterprise. It also discusses factors that may influence their likelihood of success. Challenges include access to finance and investment, recruiting and retaining talented staff, managing a social enterprise in the growth stages, and setting prices and managing cash flow. Success factors include developing a strong social network, being dedicated to the venture's success, securing seed capital, the acceptance of the venture idea in the public discourse, the ability of the service to stand the market test, and the entrepreneur's previous managerial experience. In addition to discussing the challenges and success factors, the chapter explains ways to overcome the challenges, as well as how to set the conditions needed for success.

Success Factors

Every social entrepreneur aims to be successful, but how do you define success? While some would say that success is defined by factors such as the size of the organization or the amount of gross or net revenue it generates annually, defining success in social entrepreneurship is not that simple. As organizations that aim to simultaneously alleviate social problems while engaging in entrepreneurial activities, definitions of success must include both social and economic outcomes. Table 11.1 outlines some general indicators of success. However, it should be noted that these indicators are general, standard indicators of success, but true success is defined by the entrepreneur(s) or executive board members running the organization.

In addition, because the social impact models of social enterprises can differ dramatically, there is no "one-size-fits all" approach to social impact measurement (as discussed in Chapter 9). For example, a social enterprise that collects food waste from public organizations like schools and government offices and utilizes it to make fertilizer (e.g. Re-Nuble) could measure social

DOI: 10.4324/9781003226963-12

Table 11.1 Examples of Social and Economic Indicators of Success

Social	Economic
• Number of beneficiaries served • Amount of donations received (if applicable) • Types of social issues addressed • Depth of social issues addressed • Outcomes for different stakeholders	• Gross and net annual revenue • Amount of startup funding acquired • Amount of customer interest in the organization (even if revenue is low) • Number of years established • Size of the organization

impact by the amount of pounds of food waste that it collects each month or year. However, that standard of measurement is irrelevant to a social enterprise like Warby Parker that donates one pair of glasses to a person in need for each pair that is purchased. Their social impact models are too different to truly capture the value they create in a standardized assessment.

While a multidimensional assessment of success varies by organization, in general a social enterprise is successful if it sustainably generates revenue that enables it to consistently attend to its social mission. A study of Israeli social enterprises identified common success factors among social enterprises that achieve this goal. The success factors identified include developing a strong social network, being dedicated to the venture's success, securing seed capital, the acceptance of the venture idea in the public discourse, the ability of the service to stand the market test, and the entrepreneur's previous managerial experience. Each factor is described below.

Professional and social network. A network is defined as a system or group of interconnected people or things. Networking is a powerful tool in entrepreneurship in general, but social entrepreneurship in particular because of the influence it may have on entrepreneurial and community development-related opportunities. Having a strong and diverse network helps social entrepreneurs gain access to financial, social, physical, and intellectual capital that may not otherwise be available to them. In addition, having a diverse network is important for achieving different goals. Many social enterprise beneficiaries come from historically marginalized communities. Having people in your network may help entrepreneurs convey the true need and value of their organization to their target community (cultural capital). Similarly, having government officials and other elites in your network may grant access to funding, training, and other opportunities that help legitimize and amplify the work of social enterprises (political capital).

However, on a personal note, I often attend networking events as a professor, and I must say that networking is not about trying to assess what you can get from the people you meet or as many people as possible. It's about developing positive <u>relationships</u> that have the potential to be productive and maybe even profitable. However, if you come off as someone that wants to use people, they will not like you and it could hurt your reputation. Aim to develop sincere connections with people for the long-haul. If social enterprise is a strategy for community development and community development takes time, then aim to cultivate long-term mutually beneficial relationships with people in your network. Seeking out and forming long-term connections in the sector specifically will foster success. The social enterprise community is large in the sense that it spans the globe, but in comparison to many sectors and industries (e.g. education), it is quite small.

Dedication to the social enterprise's success. Entrepreneur dedication is a hallmark of entrepreneurship, regardless of whether they are social or commercial entrepreneurs. The entrepreneurial journey is not a linear process. It is filled with twists and turns, ups and downs, successes and disappointments. A dedicated entrepreneur will rock the journey, while an uncommitted entrepreneur will *be rocked* by the inevitable difficulties they face. Entrepreneurs must be resilient, flexible, adaptable, and to an extent courageous because they will have to take calculated (but not reckless) risks throughout their journey.

Startup funding and resources. While I dislike the saying "it takes money to make money," there is some truth to it. Having the appropriate amount of startup funding and resources can remove many barriers and simplify key activities needed to launch an organization. For example, when I launched Weaver's Social Enterprise Directory, Inc. in 2018, I acquired almost $50,000 in funding, another $50,000 worth of human resources (e.g. staff), and about $5,000 for creating promotional materials and inviting social enterprise leaders to the directory launch event. It thus took about five months for me to go from idea to prototype and finding someone who could develop the minimum viable product (MVP). Were it not for that funding, it would have taken much, much longer.

This reality is why I am so passionate about this book and connecting with aspiring and early stage social entrepreneurs through my courses, bootcamps, and coaching sessions. This book aims to equip change agents with an understanding of how to acquire different community capitals needed to launch their ventures. Yes, you can launch a venture with very little resources, but you are more likely to have a strong start and a strong journey if you have the resources needed for early stage success.

The acceptance of the venture idea in the market. This success factor comes off as straightforward, but it is not. When the market likes your product or service, it manifests in sales and/or attention or activity around it. However, sometimes, social entrepreneurs are pursuing the wrong consumers. In such a case, they need a **customer segment pivot**, meaning they need to do customer discovery research to identify who will pay for their product or service. Recall in Chapter 3 that some consumers are the customers that pay for a product or services, some are simply the users of a product or service, and some are the beneficiaries of the social benefits that come from selling the product or service. This distinction between consumer types is very important and often missed among early stage entrepreneurs.

For example, a social enterprise I have partnered with for my "Social Entrepreneurship, Civic Engagement, and Community Development" course collaborated with my class for customer discovery research. They had a difficult time securing their target customers (daycare centers) for their app that aims to create an app-based support community for families that have children in daycare. Ten of my students conducted a 15-week customer discovery research project for the organization and found that their revenue model and target consumers were not appropriate for the kinds of needs their consumers have. It was also not profitable for their organization. They are now able to use this information to revamp their entire business model in a way that meets the needs of their target beneficiaries, while capturing revenue in a different way. There are other kinds of pivots (e.g. delivery channel, team, marketing) that startups may encounter so social entrepreneurs should validate their assumptions and literally do their research before assuming that their business is a failure.

The composition of the venturing team. The people on your team are critical to its success. While this may seem like common sense, it can be very difficult to turn away people that are interested in your organization yet may not be a good fit. It can also be difficult to navigate the challenges of partnership. In addition, deciding the right ratio of volunteers to salaried employees can also be a challenge. For instance, volunteers are free; however, they are more likely and able to leave the organization at any moment because they do not receive a salary. Yet, some entrepreneurs forgo having salaried employees for years to keep the organization lean until it is ready to grow. In some cases, as mentioned in Chapter 6, entrepreneurs may want to bootstrap with contract-only, temporary employees, or simply outsource specific job duties. Regardless of the option one chooses, focus on having a clear mission and direction for the organization and recruit people who are best able to help you fulfill that mission. The culture of your organization, which is influenced by the people within it and the behaviors you tolerate as an entrepreneur, is essential to your long-term success or failure.

The ability to survive the market test. The term "going to market" refers to creating an action plan for a new product, service, or organization. It may even involve re-launching an organization. While some entrepreneurs just launch products and services without researching the market, prototyping, experimenting, and creating an MVP, trained and/or informed entrepreneurs understand the value of researching the market. All consumers will not buy your product or service even if it benefits them. Some do not have the money to pay for it. Some simply will not care about it. Some will not see its value. Some may simply not know of its existence, especially in a world inundated with so many products and services.

So, some essential questions for every new social entrepreneur to ask include:

- Who will pay for the product or service (e.g. children use toys, but usually do not pay for them)?

- Who will benefit from the product or service?
- How will the social mission of a social enterprise influence consumer behavior?

These questions are important baseline questions every social entrepreneur should consider in an effort to improve their understanding of the market. Like commercial entrepreneurs, social entrepreneurs should prototype and test the market. They should expect progress to take some time and iteration (as discussed in Chapter 3). In addition, what opportunities and threats (e.g. recession, pandemic, racial tension) exist in the world that may adversely affect or positively impact the organization. Questions like this help to prepare social entrepreneurs for the context where they will operate.

The entrepreneur's previous managerial experience. I speak, engage with, and teach a great deal of entrepreneurs. One of the commonalities among some of their lessons learned include either viewing their previous managerial or industry experience as a benefit to understanding the logistics of running an organization. In addition, industry experience, even at the employee level, can help an entrepreneur understand their target market if viewed from the perspective of it being a market research opportunity.

Challenges

Challenges are inevitable in life, let alone business. However, they are often an opportunity to make necessary and productive changes. Common challenges faced by social entrepreneurs include access to finance and investment, recruiting and retaining talented staff, managing a social enterprise in the growth stages, and setting prices and managing cash flow.

The main challenges social enterprises face pertain to revenue generation, marketing, growth, and staff skills or staff size. Some of the challenges regarding revenue generation may pertain to product pricing issues. A study of social enterprises in Ireland found that many social enterprises, as socially conscious organizations, have trouble pricing products and managing cash flow, developing competitive marketing campaigns, and simply growing their organizations. In essence, some social enterprises are so passionate about combating social issues that they may over-prioritize their social goals, while losing sight of the need to generate revenue that supports their operation.

A Special Note about Failure

In addition to facing challenges, entrepreneurs will most certainly experience failure. I cannot emphasize enough the importance of *failing fast and failing forward*. It is not personal; it is a part of the entrepreneurial learning process. Some examples of failure include failing to make enough money to cover payroll, failing a pitch competition, failing to hire the right employee, and failing to successfully run the organization. Failure is so common that I feel comfortable stating that if you cannot handle failure you should not be an entrepreneur. Social entrepreneurs, in particular, may have increased chances of failing at something simply because they operate organizations with a dual mission, leaving opportunities to fail at one or both. However, learning from failure and utilizing the lessons learned to navigate throughout the entrepreneurial journey is a critical component to entrepreneurship. Entrepreneurs must have a thick skin. Most people are employees and thus do not understand an entrepreneur's experience. It is essential that entrepreneurs take care of their mental health and well-being by recognizing that failure is a learning opportunity – an opportunity for growth as opposed to a reflection of their self-worth. In some cases, failure may actually be a good thing because it may lead to an even greater opportunity.

Conclusion

Like all organizations, successful and unsuccessful social enterprises leave behind patterns that illustrate their ultimate outcomes. When social enterprises fail, it is often due to cash flow management issues, not having a solid revenue model, or issues related to recruiting and retaining quality employees. When social enterprises succeed, it is usually because they are armored with a rigid determination, a strong and productive network, have access to financing or other resources, and are educated enough to recognize when to pivot their business model to best meet the needs of their market. While success is desired, failure is common in entrepreneurship. It is essential that social entrepreneurs understand this and utilize their failures as the learning opportunities they are.

12 Social Enterprise Laws

The laws that exist today were born out of circumstances and the history of social enterprise legal structures is a good illustration of that. Social enterprises engage in entrepreneurial actions with the ambition of combatting societal problems. These goals of creating social and economic value make them hybrid organizations. They are an emerging institutional form that is blurring the boundaries of the nonprofit and private sector. Traditionally, business is defined as the activity of making, buying, or selling goods in exchange for revenue. The goal of a business is to generate revenue for the economic benefit of its owners or shareholders. However, social enterprises differ from traditional businesses in that they possess social and economic goals. They may be nonprofit organizations, for-profit businesses, or a combination of both organizational forms.

Over the last 15 years, new types of legal forms have also been developed to support the social and economic goals of social enterprises such as the Benefit Corporation, the Low-Profit Limited Liability Company (L3C), the Benefit Limited Liability Company (Benefit LLC), and the Social Purpose Corporation. These new legal forms, often referred to as hybrid laws, enable social enterprises to operate as for-profit businesses that *prioritize* their social mission over profit. They differ by the number of profits distributed to shareholders, their transparency and public reporting requirements, and the level at which they prioritize their social goals. Ultimately, all social enterprises (regardless of legal form) balance a dual bottom-line structure consisting of their social and economic goals. This chapter explores the legal structures that social enterprises operate under, the benefits and challenges of different legal structures, and how legal structure may be utilized by social entrepreneurs to best capture social and economic value in their context.

Social Enterprise Legal Structure

Social enterprise may incorporate under any legal structure. To give you an idea of just how diverse their legal structure may be, let's review results from my study of 115 social enterprises in the United States in Figure 12.1. Eighty-eight percent of social enterprises in the study are for-profit businesses.

DOI: 10.4324/9781003226963-13

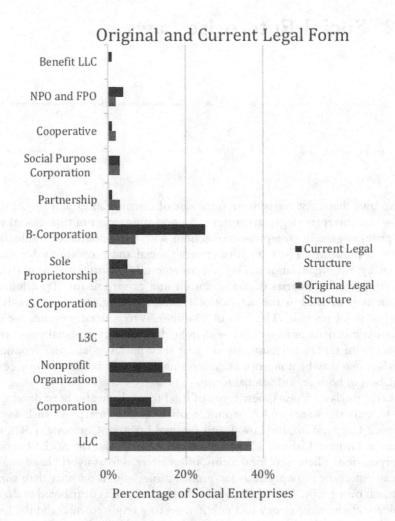

Figure 12.1 Original and Current Legal Structure.
Note: Some respondents incorporate under multiple legal forms.

Forty-one percent in the entire study incorporate under hybrid laws (e.g. Benefit Corporations). Thirty-nine percent of social enterprises solely incorporate under traditional for-profit laws (this variable excludes social enterprises that incorporate under both traditional and hybrid laws). Fourteen percent are nonprofit organizations. Take note that many social enterprises have changed their legal structure over time, especially since the development of hybrid laws. While this illustration shows data from the United States, the propensity of social enterprises that incorporate under a particular legal structure differs by country.

Social Enterprise (Hybrid) Laws

As previously mentioned throughout the book, social enterprise, as a field, emerged out of the nonprofit sector as government and philanthropic funding for nonprofit organizations decreased over time. Being that social issues continue to exist, many nonprofit organizations found themselves engaging in commercial business activities to supplement the loss of income. However, since the millennium, a new wave of organizations dedicated to running businesses with a social mission also started to increase. Earlier cases of social enterprises typically operate as for-profit businesses, nonprofit organizations, or a combination of both organizational types referred to as true hybrid organizations. However, many faced taxation and legal issues that complicated their work.

Nonprofit organizations endured the **unrelated business income tax (UBIT)** because their commercial activities did not connect with their social mission. Nonprofit organizations are required to pay UBIT when they engage in commercial activities unrelated to their charitable purpose, education, or social mission (e.g. a soup kitchen selling TVs just for profit). In addition, nonprofit organizations have a **non-distribution constraint** that requires them to re-distribute profits/surplus funds into the organization as opposed to distributing it to shareholders or owners like for-profit businesses.

For-profit businesses also have constraints. Shareholder primacy limits for-profit businesses from prioritizing their social mission because the main purpose of a traditional for-profit business is to make money. In addition, for-profit businesses are usually not eligible for philanthropic funding like nonprofit organizations. These legal, administrative, and operational challenges faced by social enterprises operating under traditional for-profit and nonprofit legal structures inspired a movement to create social enterprise laws in the early 2000s (at different time periods for different countries) to accommodate the needs of the growing number of hybrid organizations being established. Social enterprise laws, also referred to as hybrid laws, have special (self-enforced) guidelines regarding how revenue and profits are generated and utilized.

Social enterprises laws exist throughout the world. According to the Organisation for Economic Co-operation and Development (OECD), 16 countries within the European Union have adopted some kind of social enterprise law, many of which have country-specific requirements that boost social enterprise development in their context. The United States has also passed the four laws discussed in this chapter, which are also the main laws discussed in social enterprise literature. As such, there is a great deal of undiscovered and unrecorded knowledge about the influence of social enterprise law in many other countries where we know social enterprises are operating and making change. This section describes the most common social enterprise laws around the world and Table 12.1 summarizes their distinct features.

The Low-Profit Limited Liability Company (L3C) is the one of the first types of social enterprise laws to exist. L3Cs combine features from nonprofit

Table 12.1 Social Enterprise Laws

Legislation	Shareholders	Distinct Features
Low-Profit Limited Liability Company (L3C)	No	• Investors or owners may receive profits of 0%–6%. The rest must be used for Program-Related Investment (PRI).
Benefit Corporation (B-Corporation)	Yes	• Required annual financial transparency report. • Social mission is held by the standards of independent third party, but is evaluated by the shareholders and directors.
Benefit Limited Liability Company (Benefit LLC)	Varies	• Enables LLCs to re-focus mission to social.
Special Purpose Corporation (SPC)	Yes	• May prioritize socially beneficial activities over profits for shareholders.

Figure 12.2 Certified B Corp Certification Label.
Source: https://www.bcorporation.net/en-us.

organizations and for-profit businesses to meet social needs. However, like commercial businesses, L3Cs acquire funding from investors as long as investors make up to a 6% profit on their investment. The majority of profits from L3Cs must be reinvested into the business through what is called program-related investment (PRI). PRIs ensure L3Cs maintain both a social and an economic bottom-line, as commercial activities must be relevant to its social mission (Figure 12.2).

Likely the most popular social enterprise law, the Benefit Corporation (B-Corporation) law has been passed in almost every state in the United States, as well as in Italy, Columbia, parts of Canada, Ecuador, and Puerto Rico as of 2022. B-Corporation activities are directed by a group of shareholders and must have a social and/or environmental impact (Figure 12.3). For transparency purposes, B-Corporations must also provide annual reports on their performance (example shown in Figure 12.4). Benefit reports do not need to be publicly available, but may be requested. An independent third-party standard is used to guide their compliance with the law. However, compliance is monitored by shareholders and directors.

The B-Corporation is sometimes confused with B-Corp Certification, a certification process led by B Lab, a nonprofit organization that promotes B-Corporation legislation. B-Lab was created in 2006, before any type of legislation for social enterprise in the United States was passed. B-Corp Certification enables businesses throughout the world to *voluntarily* operate under specific social value-oriented conditions developed by B Lab, who evaluates these businesses using a method called *B Analytics*. While B Lab seeks to advance B-Corp legislation, it cannot pass state or federal law because it is a nonprofit organization with no governmental affiliation. B-Corp certification simply *brands* socially conscious institutions, regardless of legal form, in order to promote their social mission. As of 2022, there are over 3,500 businesses in more than 70 countries that have B-Corp Certification.

Interestingly, in 2011, the state of California in the United States established legislation for the Flexible Purpose Corporation (FPC), under its Corporate Flexibility Act. However, all FPC legislation has recently been amended to convert all FPCs into Social Purpose Corporations (SPC) in order to emphasize that they exist for social purposes. FPCs enabled for-profit private businesses to create and finance nonprofit subsidiaries that engage in charitable activities that benefit employees, suppliers, customers, the community, society, and/or the environment. However, SPCs, which were first established in Washington in 2012, are similar to the B-Corporation in that they must have a social and/or environmental mission. They differ, however, in that SPCs do not have shareholders or third-party standards for their work.

Lastly, one of the most recent types of social enterprise legislation is the Benefit Limited Liability Company (Benefit LLC). Benefit LLCs enable traditional limited liability companies to prioritize social and/or environmental causes above profit-making. The legislation enables traditional LLCs with a desire to become social enterprises to re-establish themselves in an effort to pursue socially conscious goals. Only few regions have adopted this law and little information about it exists in social enterprise literature.

These social enterprise laws were created to facilitate businesses operating with a social and economic bottom-line. However, it is essential to acknowledge that these businesses may not do so equally. Many nonprofit organizations and private businesses have converted to social enterprise legislation. Such businesses may desire to engage in both social and economic activities,

1% for the Planet

1% for the Planet*

A nonprofit we co-founded in 2002 that commits
Patagonia to donating 1% of net revenues in
cash and in-kind donations every year, primarily
to grassroots environmental nonprofits.

$116,000,000

Dollars, and dollar value of other forms of
assistance, given to support environmental work
since we started our tithing program in 1985.

$10,000,000

Dollars of donations we made on top of our 1%
commitment, using money we saved as the result of
the Trump administration's corporate tax cuts.

994

Grants funded in FY19 to 929 organizations.

450

Employees who are actively involved in grant-
making and deciding which environmental
organizations Patagonia supports.

$5,000,000+

In grants made to groups fighting to
protect lands and waters.

$400,000+

In grants made to groups working to
advance renewable energy.

$1,000,000+

In grants made to groups working to scale many of the
tenets of regenerative organic agriculture and help more
farmers implement practices to improve soil health.

Figure 12.3 Patagonia Benefit Report Page.
Source: https://www.patagonia.com/on/demandware.static/-/Library-Sites-PatagoniaShared/
default/dwf14ad70c/PDF-US/PAT_2019_BCorp_Report.pdf.

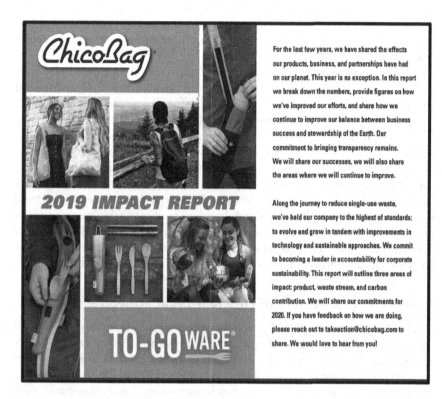

Figure 12.4 Chico Bag's Benefit Report Page.
Source: https://chicobag.com/.

but not necessarily in the equitable manner that is often (indirectly) discussed in social enterprise literature. Criticism of social enterprises operating under laws such as the B–Corporation and L3C suggests their for-profit structure makes them more susceptible to **mission drift**. Mission drift occurs when the activities of an organization differ from its original mission. The term usually applies to social enterprises that directly or indirectly prioritize their economic mission over social mission.

However, it can be argued that converting to social entrepreneurship may be mission drift for businesses that originally incorporated as for-profit businesses or nonprofit organizations. I refer to these businesses as *converted social enterprises*. A social enterprise's desired level of commercial and social activities in converted social enterprises may not empirically align with theories about social enterprise. Literature on social enterprise often assumes they are what I refer to as **constructed social enterprises**. Constructed social enterprises are designed to meet social and economic goals. Being that there is no research that examines the purpose and goals of both converted and constructed social enterprises, future studies are needed to improve theory about their influence on social and economic performance. This is particularly important due to recent research on **social and commercial imprinting**.

Social imprinting is when a social enterprise founding team places an emphasis on accomplishing the organization's social mission. **Commercial imprinting** indicates that a social enterprise emphasizes its commercial activities. Converted social enterprises should be expected to have commercial imprinting if they are for-profit businesses and social imprinting if they are nonprofit organizations. However, I suggest social enterprises may have either or both if they are constructed social enterprises. Imprinting is particularly important because it affects social performance. Social imprinting is a paradox. It weakens economic productivity because it dedicates economic and human resources to its social mission. In doing so, it inevitably weakens social performance by not increasing economic productivity. Given this research, it is essential to understand social enterprise legal form because it relates to the value of social enterprise as a tool for advancing human development.

Benefits and Challenges of Different Legal Structures

Ideally, legal structure should enable social enterprises to strategically fulfill their social impact model and revenue model within a given context. Naturally, there are strengths and weaknesses to each legal structure. For-profit social enterprises are often met with resistance, confusion, or disillusionment from people that do not believe for-profit motives and social values mix well. Nonprofit social enterprises have limitations in how they may generate revenue and re-distribute surplus funds. Hybrid laws are new and unheard of by most people. As such, many people are simply confused by the concept. Yet, all of these types of legal structures have opportunities and strengths that are helping them successfully pursue their dual goals. Table 12.2 elaborates on both the challenges and opportunities of for-profit, hybrid, and nonprofit social enterprises by legal structure.

Conclusion

Social enterprise legal structure should be viewed as a strategy that enables the organization to capture and leverage resources in its context and beyond. A nonprofit structure enables social enterprises to capture philanthropic and governmental funding, donations, and tax exemption on property, bank accounts, and more. A for-profit structure enables social enterprises to generate "unrestricted" income, attract investors who seek a return on their investment, and to maintain control of their social programs since they are not reliant on external funding. Social enterprises that operate under hybrid laws have most of the same benefits as those that incorporate as traditional for-profit businesses. However, they are designed for operating with dual

Table 12.2 Unique Challenges and Opportunities of For-Profit and Nonprofit
Social Enterprises

Social Enterprise Legal Structure	Traditional For-Profit	Hybrid Legal Structure	Nonprofit Organizations
Opportunities	• For-profit businesses aim to be self-sufficient and have no limits to revenue generation and sources. • They attract investors who want a return on their investment. • Promote efficiency and innovation. • Anticipate resistance and strategize.	• Support communities exist for some hybrid legal structures that aim to support social enterprises operating under that law (e.g. B Lab Community). • Enables unrestricted revenue generation. • Profit distribution to shareholders and owners while still prioritizing social mission. • Promote efficiency and innovation. • Anticipate resistance and strategize.	• Ability to attract volunteers, tax-deductible individual donations, and grants (private, public, and foundation). • Must comply with the non-distribution constraint • Tax-emption status on property and organizational purchases.
Challenges	• Bias exists toward businesses that engage in social activities. Some people and investors do not find them genuine or believe they are counterintuitive to their existence. As such, they are skeptical to invest in them.	• Many government agencies, investors, and banks have not heard of hybrid laws or social enterprise as a concept, making it difficult for them to invest in them. • There is market pressure to compromise on social value creation.	• The unrelated business income tax requires nonprofit organizations to pay for revenue/profits generated from non-mission-related activities. • The non-distribution constraint requires nonprofit organization to redistribute all surplus into the organization.

(Continued)

Social Enterprise Legal Structure	Traditional For-Profit	Hybrid Legal Structure	Nonprofit Organizations
	• There are market, social, and political pressures to compromise on social value creation in favor of financial performance. • Finding empathetic board members and team members who share their core values.	• Finding empathetic board members and team members who share their core values.	• Nonprofits can be heavily reliant on external funding. • Nonprofits traditionally have lower salaries and lower skilled staff than FPOs.

goals, indicating to the world and anyone that joins their organization that their social mission is priority as opposed to the maximization of profits for shareholders.

With all of this in mind, however, improvements and developments are always happening in regard to social enterprise laws because the field is still young and has a great deal of opportunity in its future. These laws are not without flaws. As we learn more about social enterprise, as a field, support systems that amplify their establishment, operation, and growth may be designed and implemented in order to amplify their work.

Resources for Further Exploration

Tools

Social Enterprise Law Tracker (United States) – https://socentlawtracker.org/#/map

Books

Honeyman, R., & Jana, T. (2019). *The B corp handbook: How you can use business as a force for good*. Berrett-Koehler Publishers.
Reiser, D. B., & Dean, S. A. (2017). *Social Enterprise Law: Trust, public benefit, and capital markets*. Oxford University Press.

Conclusion

Social Entrepreneurship: A Practical Introduction is truly a passion project. It brings together years of work, years of thoughts, years of experiences, and years of passion to make something I feel is genuinely beautiful for this growing field of entrepreneurship. It aims to create a deeper connection between contemporary commercial entrepreneurship tools and strategies to the passionate, prosocial values of social entrepreneurs. The mission of this book is to equip as many people as possible with the tools needed to make money so that they may do more good with it. With that said, this book aims to equip people with the desire to utilize social enterprises as tools for creating positive social change in their communities with the knowledge needed to accomplish their goals.

Social entrepreneurs, in essence, are people who believe in civic engagement. Research shows that social entrepreneurs have either experienced or witnessed someone experience the social problems they seek to combat. As such, they develop social enterprises as a means to advance community development. However, there are many ways to engage in social entrepreneurship without becoming a social entrepreneur, as illustrated by the social entrepreneurship career opportunities shown in Figure C.1.

Important notes to remember throughout your entrepreneurial journey

- **Identifying your strengths** as a social entrepreneur and be confident enough to outsource or hire people who are strong in areas where you are weak. Each team member should bring unique skills and contributions to the team.
- **Play your strengths, not someone else's.** It's easy to copy what others do, but there can only be one you. What do you as an individual stand for? What does or will your social enterprise specialize in?
- **Create your own definition of success.** Figure out what will make you smile, happy, and satisfied. Give yourself a goal to achieve that will nourish your soul.

DOI: 10.4324/9781003226963-14

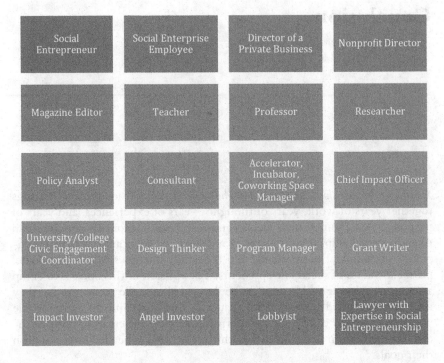

Figure C.1 Career Paths for People Interested in Social Entrepreneurship.
Source: Weaver, R. L. (2020). *Using experiential education to teach social enterprise and entrepreneurship: A teaching guide.* Association for Research on Nonprofit Organizations and Voluntary Action.

- Attempt to **obtain resources for free first**, especially in the startup phase when you are learning. Once your model has been proven to work, invest in strengthening it.
- **Save for rainy days**, as they often come "out of nowhere." Many organizations fail because they spend all of their profits. However, some profits should be saved for emergencies, as well as for innovation. You never know when the market may require your organization to pivot its business model (e.g. COVID-19 pandemic).
- **Quality over quantity.** Having a great deal of products is nice, but doubling down on your best sellers is wise. Give your consumers what you know they desire, but also spontaneously introduce new products over time to test how they are received and to keep things spicy.
- **Faith, support, and loyalty are needed in difficult times**. Anyone and everyone will support you when you are successful, but hold sacred the people there for you in your most difficult moments.

- **Play the long game** by remembering that small wins over time add up to big results. Success does not happen overnight. Also, consistent success over a period of time also demonstrates longevity, which is important for attracting investors.
- **Failure is common in entrepreneurship**. Know that you will fail at some point and know that it is a learning experience.
- **Entrepreneurs are rare** and social entrepreneurs are even more rare. Know that your vision for the world exists in your mind for a reason and do not expect others to share it. It's *your* vision for a reason. Believe that you can make your dreams come true, put the action needed to turn your ideas into reality, and you most likely will succeed.
- **Good karma keeps the blessings coming**. Whether or not you believe in karma or blessings, it is undeniably true that being a good leader and business partner will lead to good relationships with others. Don't burn bridges when you can build them, but know when to walk away from people and places that are not good for you.
- **Slow progress is still progress.** It may take years before your venture aligns with your definition of success, but it'll make the journey sweeter.

Discussion Questions for Educators

Description: The questions in this section may be used as a resource to facilitate classroom discussions about each chapter for educators and trainers.

Chapter 1: What Is Social Entrepreneurship?

1   What do we mean by the "social" in social entrepreneurship? Is there such a thing as non-social entrepreneurship? Are "all" businesses socially beneficial?
2   Why is it important to have a distinct field called social entrepreneurship?
3   What are your thoughts on having a dual or triple bottom-line? Is it feasible, practical, and ideal?
4   What are your thoughts regarding the impact of social enterprises?

Chapter 2: The Emergence of Social Enterprise Across the World

1   What are some reasons that social enterprise activity is higher in regions where there are weaker social enterprise ecosystems for that kind of work?
2   Social entrepreneurship is thought to be the future of business. Based on what you learned in Chapter 2, what kinds of opportunities are available for people seeking to enter this field?
3   Are there any other kinds of supports that social entrepreneurs can use that are not outlined in this chapter?

Chapter 3: Assessing Needs to Create Value

1   Why is it important to assess social needs in a given community before developing a social enterprise?
2   Why is it important to understand the needs and differences between different social enterprise consumer types?
3   How does the cultural and emotional state of a consumer influence their purchases?

Chapter 4: Social Enterprise and Community Development

1   What are some differences that may occur in social enterprises that have a place-based sense of community and those that have an issue-based sense of community?
2   How do social enterprises strive to have a reciprocal relationship with their community?
3   Why are the three main factors that make up a productive opportunity space valuable together, but not necessarily on their own?
4   If you started a social enterprise, what community capitals would you use?

Chapter 5: Models of Social Impact

1   What are the strengths and weaknesses of each social impact model?
2   What social impact models address issues directly impacting individuals? What models address social issues at a community-based level? What social impact models address issues at a systemic level?
3   What social problems are of major importance to you? What social impact model would you consider using to solve it?

Chapter 6: Startup Financing

1   How does startup funding help social entrepreneurs?
2   Are there occasions when it may hurt a social entrepreneur to receive startup funding? If so, please explain.
3   What are some ways you would finance a social enterprise? Would you use traditional financing, grassroots, or both and why?
4   Which seems harder/easier to acquire, traditional or grassroots financing?
5   What are some ways that you would bootstrap your social venture?

Chapter 7: Revenue Models

1   What is the difference between revenue and profit?
2   Why is it important to have a revenue model as opposed to simply knowing how you may generate revenue?
3   What is the importance of having an emergency fund/financial reserve in business? Do you think many businesses have such funds?

Discussion Questions to Explore for Business Planning?

1   Can your idea generate revenue?
2   What can you sell in order to generate revenue?
3   How many units do you need to sell in order to be profitable?

4   What happens if it takes a while (e.g. five years) to make a profit?
5   How long do you see yourself running this business?
6   How much are customers willing to pay for your products and services?
7   How many customers do you need in order to break even?
8   How much revenue can you generate through sales?
9   If there are multiple streams of revenue, how much will you need from each to break even or to make a profit?

Chapter 8: Business Planning and Launching

1   Is all social change positive? Why or why not?
2   What is a theory of positive social change?
3   What are the strengths and weaknesses of using lean business model canvases vs. traditional business plans?
4   Is it better to start with a business plan and then launch a social enterprise or to launch and then plan based on what you learn from launching?
5   In your opinion, is anything missing from the Social Enterprise Operational Checklist? Why or why not?

Chapter 9: Social Impact Measurement

1   Do you feel that it is important for social enterprises to measure their impact? Why or why not?
2   Does social impact measurement actually help social enterprises communicate their value? If so, what kind of value?
3   What are the pros and cons of using quantitative vs. qualitative social impact measurement tools?

Chapter 10: Scaling Social Enterprise

1   What are some ways social entrepreneurs can scale their impact?
2   What organizational, contextual, and economic factors can hinder scaling a social enterprise?
3   How would you scale your social enterprise idea?

Chapter 11: Challenges and Success Factors

1   What are some ways that social enterprise success may be defined?
2   How can social entrepreneurs place themselves in a position to achieve most if not all success factors discussed in Chapter 11?
3   The main challenges social enterprises face pertain to revenue generation, marketing, growth, and staff skills or staff size. Why do you think this is a challenge for social enterprises in particular? How can they overcome this challenge?
4   What does it mean to "fail fast and fail forward?"

Chapter 12: Social Enterprise Laws

1   How can different legal structures be used as a strategy for maximizing a social enterprise's social and economic goals?
2   What are some reasons that social enterprises may change their legal structure over time?
3   How may the current social enterprise legal structures be improved to advance social entrepreneurship?

Index

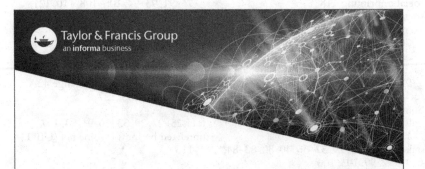

Taylor & Francis Group
an **informa** business

Taylor & Francis eBooks

www.taylorfrancis.com

A single destination for eBooks from Taylor & Francis
with increased functionality and an improved user
experience to meet the needs of our customers.

90,000+ eBooks of award-winning academic content in
Humanities, Social Science, Science, Technology, Engineering,
and Medical written by a global network of editors and authors.

TAYLOR & FRANCIS EBOOKS OFFERS:

A streamlined
experience for
our library
customers

A single point
of discovery
for all of our
eBook content

Improved
search and
discovery of
content at both
book and
chapter level

REQUEST A FREE TRIAL
support@taylorfrancis.com

 Routledge
Taylor & Francis Group

 CRC Press
Taylor & Francis Group

Printed in the United States
by Baker & Taylor Publisher Services

Printed in the United States
by Baker & Taylor Publisher Services